Music Making

Music Making

by George Seltzer

McFarland & Company, Inc.,
Publishers
Jefferson, North Carolina, and London

Library of Congress Cataloguing-in-Publication Data

Seltzer, George, 1924–
Music making.

Includes index.
1. Music—Manuals, text-books, etc. 2. Music—Theory, Elementary. I. Title.
MT7.S377 1983 781 83-42897

ISBN 0-89950-081-1 (pbk.)

Manufactured in the United States of America

Preface

Music Making is about making music. It is not about writing a hit tune—although it could be. It is not about writing a symphony—although it could be. It is about the tools and techniques used to make the music of Western culture.

Music Making is not designed as a music theory text for the preprofessional student. Rather, it is for all those who have an interest in learning how music is organized—who want to learn what makes the music machine "go"—who want to know more than the correct fingerings for a piano piece or a guitar accompaniment.

After certain basic concepts are presented, the focus of each chapter is a short composition using the tools of music most recently discussed. These compositions are performed for the class on a regular basis and serve as a means of introducing (and developing) ideas about melody, meter, harmony, form, phrasing and performance practice.

Each chapter contains a variety of "practice and development" material. Written exercises, compositions to be analyzed, listening suggestions and ear training studies, along with the composition, are meant to explore in depth a certain tool or technique of music making. Instructors should feel free to add or subtract from this material in any way they see fit.

In the many years of teaching the course upon which this text is based, I have been continually gratified by the great numbers of talented and creative persons we have among us. In fact, students learn rapidly from the creative compositional efforts of their peers—who are the real teachers of my course—and I have learned along with them each year.

I am very grateful to my colleague, Joseph H. Bein, who read my manuscript with great care and made many worthwhile suggestions. Another colleague, John F. Hardy, offered much encouragement and advice for which I am most appreciative.

My special thanks go to my students who "learned" me this course over the years.

Table of Contents

I. A Short Aural History of Western Music

Emphasizing the 18th–20th Centuries

Through an understanding of the "nuts and bolts" of musical composition in Western culture in the 18th and 19th centuries and their expansion in our own time, the reader's ability to make music will be developed. Artistic results can be expected almost as a matter of course.

In a very short time the perception of these tools of music making will lead to original composition. Each week or so, after discussion and aural illustration, your own compositions will utilize a new musical device. The performance of the music on a regular schedule will quickly build your musical resources and will help you learn many other related musical facts.

Even before we consider the characteristics of sound—our first and most important tool of music making—let's listen to a concise history of Western music. The most important aspect of this book is not in the book. It is the sound of music. Before we can begin to make out own music, we need to hear and understand the music of our great composers. We need to hear the music of the past so we can better appreciate the music of the present and future.

The verbalization of a history of music is of relatively little value to those who want to make music. The *music itself* is of the greatest importance. The following section can be a meaningless sequence of words unless musical examples of each style and period can be heard accompanying the text. With the instructor to point out what goes on in the composition, the development of Western music should be readily apparent.

The beginnings belong to prehistoric times. What we know of the ancient civilizations of Egypt, Babylonia and Sumer testify to the fact that music was already a highly developed art. The Bible frequently refers to the availability and power of music. The walls of Jericho fall to the sound of trumpets and David sings and plays the lyre.

Although the earliest known musical notation dates from 2000 B.C. and Greek and Roman references abound, only a few fragments of this early music have survived.

Recording: Mesomedes of Crete. *Hymn to the Sun* (A.D. 130)
(2000 Years of Music, Folkways 3700)*

The music of the early Christian church was influenced greatly by the still earlier Greek, Syrian and Hebrew music. This plainsong (or plainchant, or Gregorian chant) is single-line (i.e., monophonic) music with a subtle rhythm dependent upon the text.

Recording: *Alleluia: Vidimus stellam*
(Masterpieces of Music before 1750,
Haydn Society, 79038)

The over 3000 plainsongs were codified during the reign of Pope Gregory I (590–604) but it was not until around 1000 that these chants were written down in a consistent, meaningful notation. In the more than 1000 years that these melodies were handed down from mouth to ear they developed a smoothness—a flow—of melody and rhythm unmatched in our culture. They are truly the "music of the centuries."

In the codification of these chants (590–604) the melodies were classified according to modes. These eight scale-like patterns called "church modes" are the melodic and harmonic foundation of over 1000 years of Western art music. This "modal" structure would not be supplanted until around 1600.

Sometime close to the 9th century, the most important development in Western music occurred when a second part was added to the Gregorian chant. This simple parallel structure (called *organum*) was the beginning of polyphony—the use of more than one musical sound at the same time. It made Western music forever different from the music of all other cultures. Polyphony forced the development of a system of pitch notation and when the individual voices began to develop more independence, rhythmic notation was a necessity as well.

During the hundreds of years that polyphony was developing, the preponderance of both sacred and secular music was still monophonic.

Recording: Raimbaut de Vagueiras. *Kalenda Maya* (1195)
(Music of the Middle Ages—Lyrichord LL 85)

**The records listed here are merely suggestions. The instructor may well substitute others. "Hard-to-find" recordings are identified with a record company and number.*

The mass, as the central ritual of the Roman Catholic church, has attracted composers for some 800 years. The music of the medieval church used Gregorian chant as an integral part in the construction of new compositions. This *cantus firmus* (fixed song) chant may not be perceptible to the listener but it served admirably as both a symbolic and formal support for the new polyphonic composition.

Recording: Guillaume de Machaut. *Mass of Notre Dame*
(before 1364): "Agnus Dei"
(Bach Guild B.G. 622)

The rapid development of polyphonic techniques along with an improved system of rhythmic notation brought music into the Renaissance. Although a late blooming art, in the latter part of the 15th century music was able to take its rightful place with the other fine arts of the Renaissance age.

The music of the early Renaissance used imitative techniques and—for the first time—harmonic structures and progressions that "make sense" to the 20th century ear.

Recording: Josquin des Prez. Motet: *O Domine Jesu Christe*
(Everest 310)

The 16th century remains "the golden age of vocal polyphony," a time when fluid, graceful, flowing melodies were skillfully interwoven into a web of continuous imitation. A time when sacred and secular music were of equal importance. The mass and the madrigal give comparable pleasure.

Recording: Giovanni Pierluigi da Palestrina.
Pope Marcellus Mass: "Gloria"

Recording: Thomas Morley. *Arise, Awake*
(Madrigal Guild, Triumphs of Oriana Music
Library, MLR 7002)

The change in any art form from one era to another is in part due to a revolt against the old ways by the artist. With the beginnings of the Baroque era (around 1600 to 1750) there is a shift from music with several independent parts of equal importance to music with a single melodic line with chordal accompaniment. Instead of the interweaving of several melodies we have a new emphasis upon what might be called the "vertical" aspect of music, with chords indicated by a bass note and figures along with the melody in an upper part. This "figured bass" or *basso continuo* or "thorough bass" was a hallmark of Baroque music; the era is sometimes known as the "thorough bass period."

With this new responsiveness to a progression of chords, a complete harmonic organization soon developed. The old church modes were replaced by just two scale types, the major and minor. These "survivors" of the modes established a system of tonality so pervasive that it controlled Western music during the 18th and 19th centuries and still exerts its influence in the 20th.

Inherent in this major-minor tonality is the material for contrast so vital to Western music: the contrast between the dominant (the sound of action) and the tonic (the sound of rest), the contrast between major and minor tonality. The Baroque composer added the contrast between loud and soft.

Just as the Renaissance composer emphasized rhythm to a greater extent than earlier musicians, the Baroque era valued a strong, regular beat still more. The steady, pronounced pulse of Baroque music—aided by the chordal structure of the *basso continuo*—is as much a characteristic of the period as figured bass itself.

Recording: Henry Purcell. *Dido and Aeneas*: "Dido's Lament" (Act III) (L'Oiseau-Lyre SOL 60047)

Recording: Antonio Vivaldi. *Concerto for Flute, Oboe, and Bassoon in g minor*, F. XII, no. 4

Recording: Johann Sebastian Bach. *Fugue in G minor* (the "Little," BWV 578)

Recording: Johann Sebastian Bach. *Brandenburg Concerto no. 2 in F Major* (BWV 1047): first movement

Recording: George Friedrich Handel. *Messiah*: "Hallelujah"

All the arts seem to shift periodically from periods emphasizing romantic qualities to those when classic elements predominate. The Classic period in music (from roughly 1770 to 1825), as exemplified by the music of Haydn, Mozart, Beethoven and Schubert, stressed objectivity, clarity, balance, logic and reason as contrasted with the romantic qualities of subjectivity, emotionalism and sentimentality. In this sense both the music of the Baroque and the 19th century can be described as "Romantic."

The Baroque composer's musical vocabulary included imitative techniques, terraced dynamics (i.e., music which becomes suddenly loud or soft), passages exhibiting a single "affect" or feeling, and dependence upon thorough bass and the improvisation and virtuosity of performers.

The Classic composer enlarged his vocabulary by a greater development of the major-minor system, the use of crescendo and decrescendo and the perfection of a musical form, which, enabled him to manipulate material in a section of development. This musical form—the sonata—was a concept that served as a model for 18th, 19th and 20th century composers. The principle of the sonata cycle brought forth compositions for solo performance, trios, quartets, solo with orchestra (the concerto) and finally the sonata for full orchestra—the symphony.

Recording: Wolfgang Amadeus Mozart. *Eine Kleine Nachtmusik*: third movement, "Minuet"

Recording: Franz Josef Haydn. *String Quartet in C Major*, op. 76, no. 3 (the "Emperor"): second movement

Recording: Ludwig Van Beethoven. *Symphony no. 1 in C Major*, op. 21: first movement

Recording: Ludwig Van Beethoven. *Sonata for Piano in c minor*, op. 13 (the "Pathetique"): third movement

Aaron Copland, one of the very important 20th century composers, reminds us of the basic principle of repetition in Western music, Copland says: "It [repetition] is so fundamental to the art that it is likely to be used in one way or another as long as music is written."*

The procedure of presenting a section of music followed by a contrasting section and followed again by a repetition of the original material (A–B–A) seems to satisfy an important need in Western people. In fact, one of our most popular forms in music is A–A–B–A. In other words, we are perfectly happy to listen to a work three fourths of which is repetition!

The various forms of Western music from whatever century, for the great part, utilize this "contrast-repetition" structure. Whether the form is rondo, variations, fugue or sonata this principle applies. It is as meaningful in a 13th century motet as in a 20th century ballet.

What identifies 19th century Romanticism in music? Besides the improvement in performers and instruments, composers shifted their emphasis from objectivity, balance and clarity to subjectivity, emotionalism and personal involvement. Compositions became longer and louder and called for huge orchestras and choruses. Tone color (or timbre) and innovative harmonic structures became almost an end in themselves. At the same time, the so-called "small forms"—the short piano piece and the art song—are also representative of this century. Program music (music that "tells a story" or "paints a picture") and nationalism (compositions associated with patriotism) are still other aspects of 19th century Romanticism.

Recording: Franz Schubert. *Erlkonig*, op. 1

Recording: Frederic Chopin. *Prelude in e minor*, op. 28, no. 4

Recording: Bedrich Smetana. *The Moldau*

Recording: Richard Wagner. *Tristan und Isolde*: "Prelude"

*What to Listen For in Music *(New York: McGraw-Hill, 1939), page 69.*

No transition from one musical style to another is abruptly accomplished on a single date or year. The beginnings of what we call 20th century music grew logically from 19th century romanticism. And as in all other transitional periods, there were mixtures of conservative and progressive techniques existing at the same time.

Impressionism is probably both an extension of 19th century Romanticism and an introduction to the 20th century. This "stretching" of tonality and the search for new ways to create music (many times utilizing very old musical styles) opened the road to a great diversity of attitudes and directions of composition. Among the many tracks serious 20th century music explores are an expansion of tonality unheard of in previous times, the negation of tonality and the development of polytonal centers, the introduction of the 12-tone technique and eventually total serialism (which is a mechanistic control of other aspects of music—timbre, rhythm, dynamics, etc.—in the same way the pitch is controlled in a "tone row"), the development of new and complex rhythmic structures, and the deliberate effort of the composer to abstain from composing—that is, the introduction of "chance" or aleatory music.

And then came electronic music. The composer now deals with new music-making machines that can produce *exact* pitches, dynamics, timbres, rhythms. These musical elements can then be "manipulated" by tape-recording them and using them at half speed, double speed or backwards. Since we are now in the computer age, it is also possible to come to a computer terminal with a notebook in hand, "feed" the computer the compositional material and leave the terminal with a musical composition forever complete on a tape. All this, for the first time in history, without the musical talents of a performer.

At the same time 20th century music encompasses also the blues, ragtime, jazz, rock 'n' roll, country-western and musical theatre. All these styles are a direct continuation and expansion of 19th century "common practice" tonality and tradition-based forms with innovative rhythmic procedures.

Recording: Claude Debussy. *Nocturnes. Nuages*

Recording: Igor Stravinsky. *Rite of Spring. Sacrificial Dance*

Recording: Arnold Schoenberg. *Five Pieces for Orchestra*, op. 16

Recording: Edgard Varèse. *Ionisation*

Recording: George Crumb. *Ancient Voices of Children*

Recording: *Music of Our Time: A Guide to the Electronic Revolution in Music*
(CBS)

II. Characteristics of Sound
Pitch, Volume, Timbre, Duration

The most important tool for making music is sound itself. Music is continuously concerned with *pitch* (how high or low is a sound), *volume* (how loud or soft is a sound), *timbre* (how a sound "sounds"—its tone quality) and *duration* (how long or short is a sound).

Let's first consider *pitch*. Sound is caused by vibrations. Musical sound is caused by regular (or periodic) vibrations. The pitch of a sound is related to the frequency (speed) of these vibrations—the greater the frequency, the higher the pitch. Frequency is sometimes referred to as "cps" (cycles per second). For example, a violin has a pitch range from a low of approximately 300 cps to a high of approximately 3000 cps.

Volume is related to the size (or amplitude) of the vibrations produced by the sound source. The greater the amplitude of the vibrations, the louder we perceive the sound—and conversely.

The same pitch produced by a piano, violin or clarinet sounds differently. This difference is in *timbre*, or tone quality. All musical instruments create different timbres because the sound wave they cause is made up of a fundamental (the pitch we recognize) and several other weaker pitches above this fundamental called overtones, or partials. Each instrument (except electronic sound-generating machines which can make "pure" sounds) has its own characteristic "spectrum" or harmonic series made up of a fundamental and partials of varying numbers and strengths.

Example 1 contains the harmonic series built on the fundamental C. And this brings us to another important aspect of pitch. When we visualize a rainbow we are aware of a continuous blending of one color into another for

1. Harmonic Series

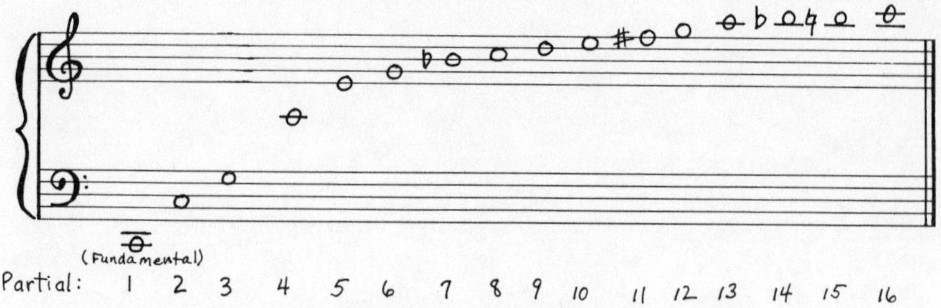

the entire visual spectrum. There is a similar aural spectrum of frequency throughout our hearing range. Musical pitches, however, are discrete. That is, for the most part Western music deals with pitches that are never closer together than a certain minimum number of vibrations.

All cultures seem to recognize the "sameness" of the octave. The similarity of two pitches an octave apart makes it the basic interval in music. And, as Example 1 illustrates, the octave is the first interval in the harmonic series. This physical characteristic of sound parallels a universal cultural value.

Musical cultures differ in how the octave is divided. Western music, certainly from the 18th century, has been based upon the division of the octave into 12 equally spaced pitches. These 12 pitches repeated through all the octaves of our hearing range constitute all the "pitch material" available for the thousands of compositions created in the 18th, 19th and a good part of the 20th centuries. This time span is sometimes called "the common practice period"—a long period of time in which Western composers used and further developed the same tools of music making.

2. Western Music's Chromatic Scale of 12 Pitches

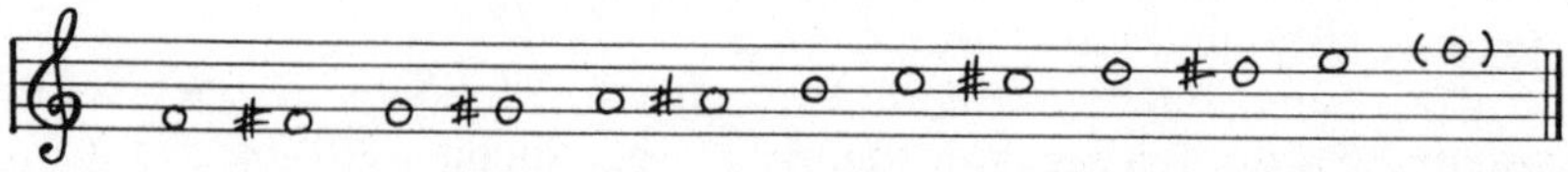

In large part, the nuts and bolts of music making are the discovery and utilization of the many relationships of these 12 pitches. These relationships are important because, after all, we probably have fewer than 100 useful pitches available (the piano keyboard has 88) and many compositions use fewer than 50.

Although the length of time a sound lasts, its *duration*, is a physical characteristic of sound, it probably will be more useful to approach this aspect when we discuss concepts in the organization of time (Chapter IV). It is sufficient to note here that just as sounds can differ in pitch, volume and timbre, so can they differ in duration.

Exercises

1. Listen to various instruments (including voice) produce the same pitch. Can you distinguish among them?

And for those who are familiar with music notation:

2. Reproduce the harmonic series to the 16th partial on the following fundamental pitches: G, F, D.

3. The sixth partial of the fundamental A is ________.
   The fourth partial of the fundamental E is ________.

4. Reproduce a chromatic scale for two octaves beginning on: D, B♭.

Listening Assignment

Schubert. *String Quartet* in a minor, op. 29

Pachebel. *Cannon a' 3 on a Ground in D Major*

3. *Musical Notation and the Piano Keyboard*

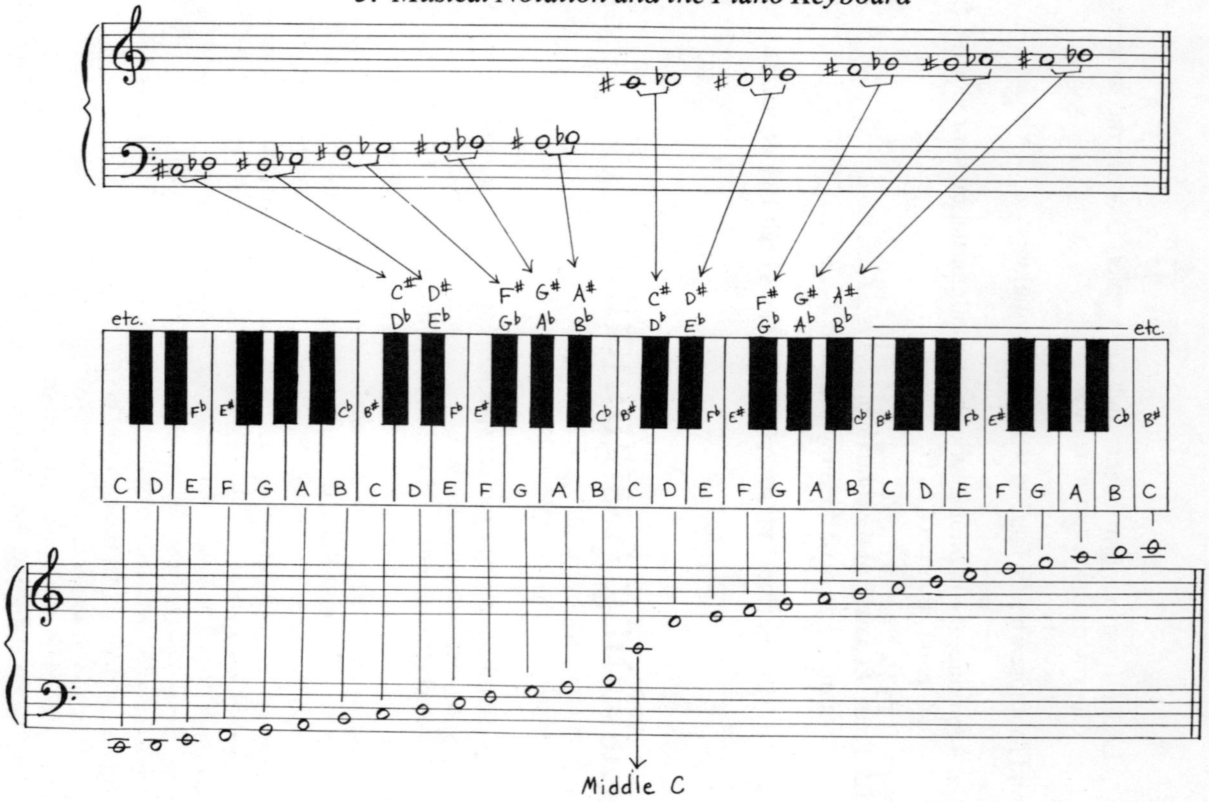

III. Pitch Relationships
Major and Minor Scales; The Circle of Fifths; Key Signatures; Intervals

The music of the 17th, 18th, 19th and a good part of the 20th centuries is based on the major and minor scales—the two survivors of the much older church modes.

Before we analyze these scales it will be helpful to associate our written musical notation with the piano keyboard. Example 3 (opposite) not only reproduces the piano keyboard but also illustrates the "pitch space" occupied by any particular note on our double staff. The upper staff is identified by the treble clef, the upper device at the left edge of the two staves of music in Example 3. The lower staff is identified by the bass clef, the lower of the two devices. The two staffs "join" at middle C and proceed in either direction with our seven-lettered musical alphabet. From the clef signs we can deduce the name of each line and space of the staffs. We need additional symbols to indicate still smaller pitch distances. The sharp (♯) raises a pitch (see the relationship in Example 3 on the keyboard between the white key "F" and the black key "F♯"). The flat (♭) lowers a pitch (see the relationship in the example on the keyboard between the white key "A" and the black key "A♭"). Piano keys with two names (for instance, F♯ is also G♭ and G♯ is also A♭) are notationally different on the staff and are called "enharmonic."

Let's look again at the chromatic scale, which simply utilizes the 12 pitches possible in our standard notation.

The pitch distance between each of these notes is a semitone or halftone (or half-step). This is the smallest possible pitch distance, or "interval," in our standard notation.

4. The Chromatic Scale

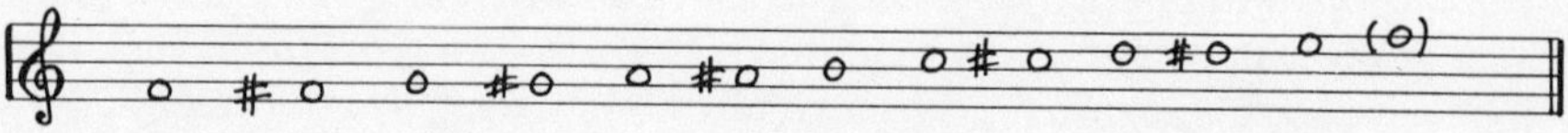

Now that we are aware that the semitone is the smallest interval, we can investigate the major scale with more understanding.

5. The Major Scale

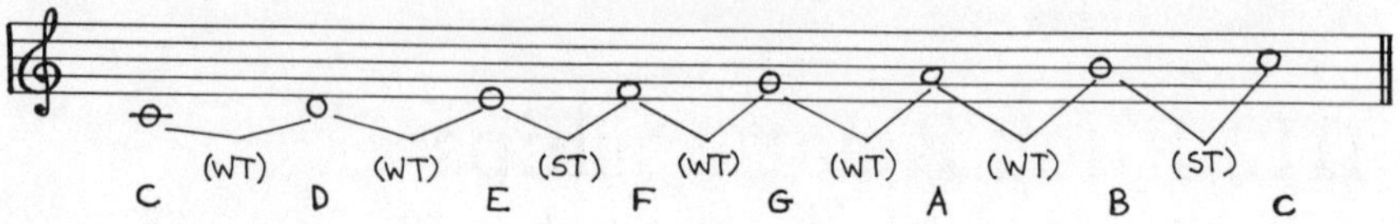

The major scale illustrated in Example 5 is called the C Major scale because the sequence of pitches begins on C. It is obvious from our knowledge of the semitone that this scale is not simply a set of equally spaced notes. Example 5 shows that there is a whole tone (WT), equal to the space of two semitones, between C and D, D and E, F and G, G and A and A and B. There is a semitone (ST) between E and F and between B and C.

In other words, the intervallic relationship that creates what we call a major scale is: WT, WT, ST, WT, WT, WT, ST. It is interesting to note again the basic importance of the octave relationship. The major scale contains only seven different tones, the eighth—the octave (from the Latin *octo*, "eight")—takes the same "name" as the first.

6. The Major Scale

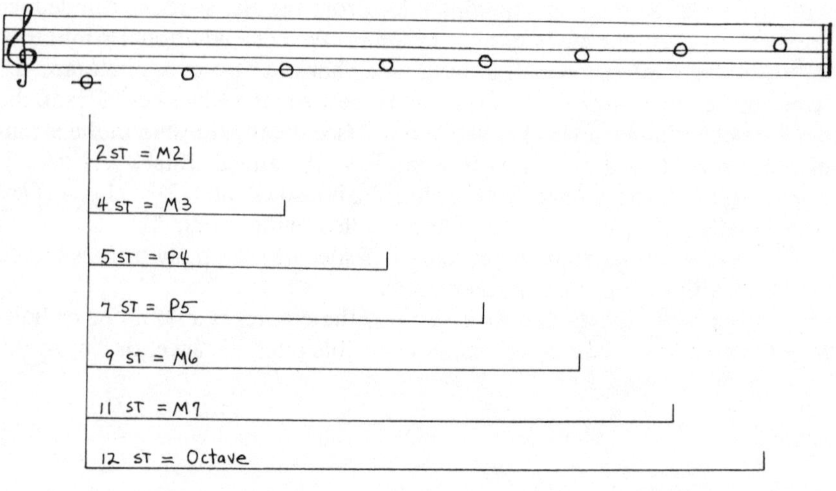

Example 6 gives us another interesting way to view the intervallic relationships within a major scale. Once we can associate the semitone with pitch distance in the same way we think of the inch with space distance, it is a simple matter to measure the distance between pitches in a major scale.

We call the distance of two semitones a major second (2 ST = M2) just as we call 12 inches a foot. Similarly four semitones equal a major third (4 ST = M3), five semitones equal a perfect fourth (P4), and so on.

Now we have another set of intervallic relationships that create the same major scale: M2, M3, P4, P5, M6, M7, Octave.

Once we know the intervallic relationships that create what we call a major scale, we can produce that specific sound pattern at any pitch level. For example, to form a major scale beginning on G or F we need only to duplicate the WT–ST pattern of Example 5 or the M2, M3, P4, P5, M6, M7 Octave pattern of Example 6.

7. G and F Major Scales

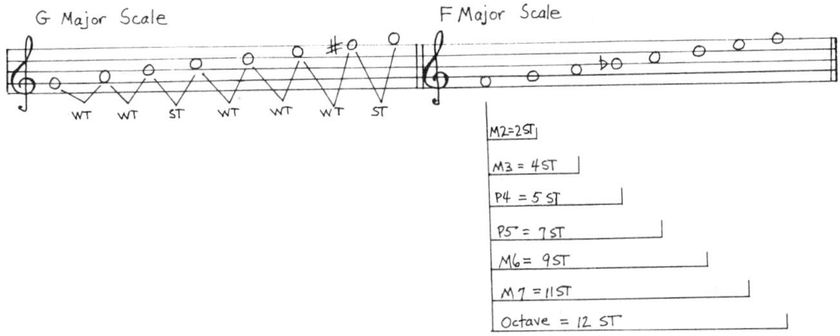

Thc G and F Major scales in Example 7 use a sharp and a flat, respectively, to form the intervallic pattern we associate with the sound of a major scale. It follows that as we use other pitches as starting points of this major scale sound, other sharps or flats will be used. In a composition written in G Major, every F would have to become an F♯. To avoid this mechanical reproduction of the sharp each time, notation has a predictable sort of shorthand. This system is called "key signatures" and entails the placement of the needed sharps or flats only at the beginning of each musical line.

8. Major Key Signatures

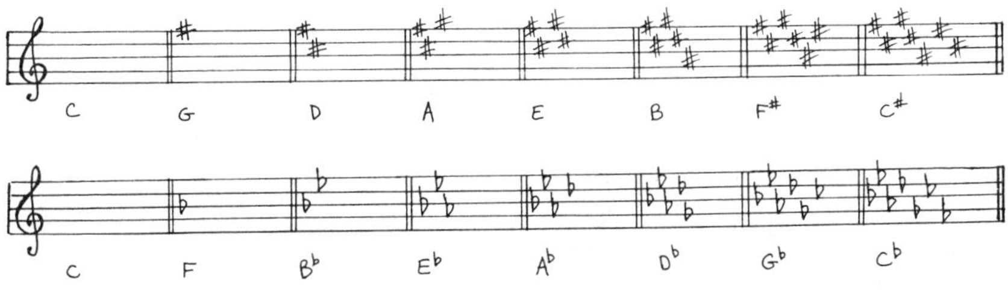

There are several points of interest in Example 8.

1. As the new key center *ascends* a P5 (e.g., C to G, G to D, etc.) a sharp is added to the key signature.
2. Each sharp is added at the intervallic relationship or an *ascending* P5 (e.g., F♯ to C♯ to G♯, etc.).
3. As the new key center *descends* a P5 (e.g., C to F, F to B♭, etc.) a flat is added to the key signature.
4. Each flat is added at the intervallic relationship of a *descending* P5 (e.g., B♭ to E♭ to A♭, etc.).

This information "gives" us the key signature for any major scale. All we need do is count the number of perfect fifths (P5's) the key center is removed from C and add the same number of sharps or flats beginning with either F♯ or B♭. Rote memorization of key signatures is not necessary. For example: to obtain the key signature for A Major, simply add P5's above C (C–G–D–A = 3 P5) and place three sharps in the key signature beginning with F♯ and continuing upwards by P5 (F♯–C♯–G♯); to obtain the key signature for B♭ Major, simply add P5's down from C (C–F–B♭ = 2 P5) and place two flats in the key signature beginning with B♭ and continuing downwards by P5 (B♭–E♭).

9. The Circle of Fifths—Major Scales

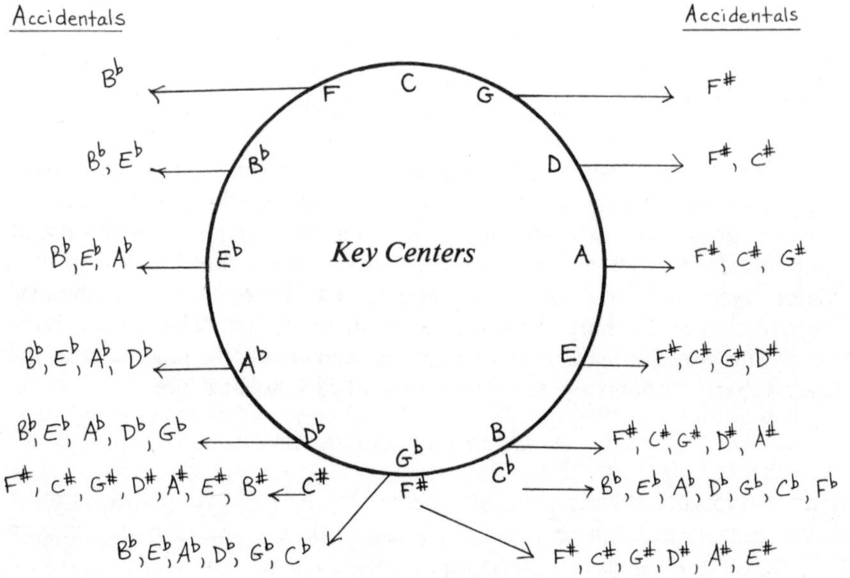

The same concept is illustrated in Example 9. The graphic representation of the "circle of fifths" agrees with the information given in Example 8. Note the "overlapping" of the key centers D♭–C♯, F♯–G♭ and B–C♭.

These key centers are "enharmonic" (see Example 3) and will be reproduced on the keyboard using the identical keys.

The major scale is complemented by—or contrasted with—the minor scale. Although there is only one set of intervallic relationships possible for the sound pattern of a major scale, there are various forms of the minor scale used in Western music.

The important distinction between the major and all minor scales is the location of the third step of the scale. All minor scales use the intervallic distance of a *minor* third between the first and third steps of the scale. The major scale used the major third (see examples 6 and 7).

The upper parts of the various minor scales take different forms.

10. Scale Formations Built on a

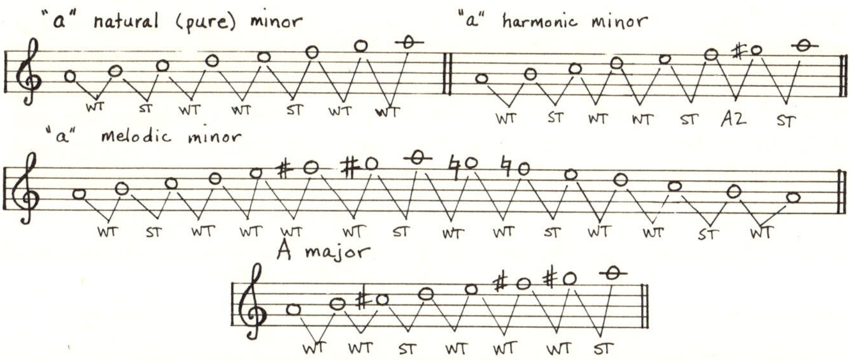

Example 10 illustrates three forms of the minor scale contrasted with the major scale. The pitch, a, was chosen because the use of just the white keys of the piano will produce the sound pattern of the natural minor scale beginning on a. All three forms of the a minor scale contain C natural (c♮ – contrasted with the C♯ in A Major), which is the distinctive lowered third of all minor scales. The natural minor scale contains a pattern of WT and ST different from that of the major scale. Since no accidentals are used to produce this sound pattern beginning on a, it will use the same key signature as C Major—no sharps or flats. Because of this commonality of pitches, C Major and a minor (*all* a minor scales) are said to be relative scales. That is, the relative minor of C Major is a and the relative major of a minor is C.

The harmonic minor and natural minor scales contain identical intervallic patterns except for the seventh step, which in the harmonic minor scale is raised, bringing it closer to the key center. This adjustment of one pitch by only a semitone accomplishes two important objectives—it creates the distinctive interval of the augmented second (three semitones) between the sixth and seventh steps and it mirrors the intervallic relationship of the major scale between the seventh step and the key note (or octave).

The melodic minor scale is unique in that it contains different intervallic relationships in its ascending and descending forms. The ascending form of the melodic minor is identical to A Major (except for the lowered-third-C), while the descending form of the scale is identical to that of the natural minor.

As with the major scale, the minor scales can be constructed on any pitch as long as the *intervallic relationships* are kept constant. With 12 different pitches available in our standard notation it is of course possible to create 12 minor scales as well as 12 major scales.

11. The Circle of Fifths—Major and Minor Scales

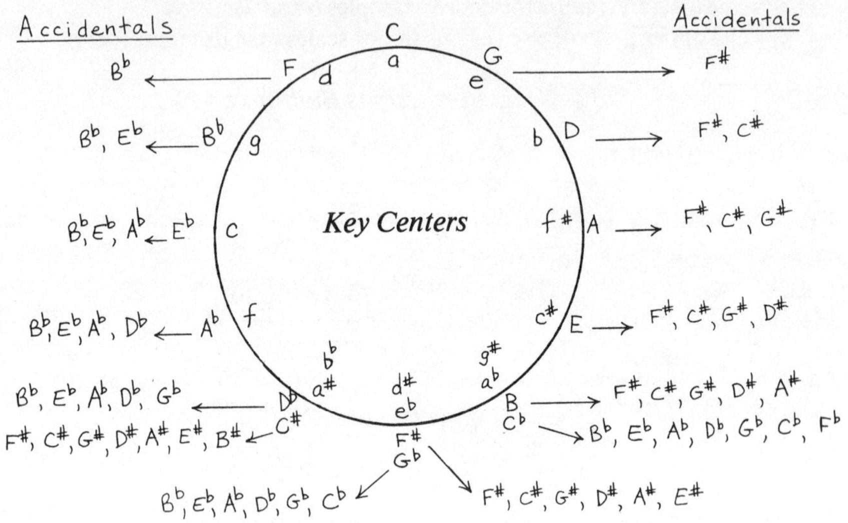

Example 11 contains the same circle of fifths as in Example 9 with the addition of the minor scales. Although the relative major and minor scales use the same key signature (e.g., C Major and a minor, E♭ Major and c minor, A Major and f♯ minor), because of imperfections in our notational system it is always necessary to make mechanical (and repeated) adjustments with individual accidentals when the harmonic or melodic forms of the minor scale are used.

Another intervallic relationship seems important to note here. The pitch space between a major scale and its relative minor is always three semitones downward (a minor third). This fact makes the use of the circle of fifths still easier. For example, if we know the key signature for A♭ Major, the same key signature is used for f minor (a minor third below A♭ Major); if we know the key signature for c minor, the same key signature is used for E♭ Major (a minor third above c minor).

In many cases it is cumbersome to refer to intervallic relationships in terms of semitones and whole tones. Although we could identify a yard as equal to 36 inches, we are much more likely to say it equals three feet. Similarly, it is more convenient to refer to a major third than four semitones or two whole tones.

12. *Common Intervals in Standard Notation*

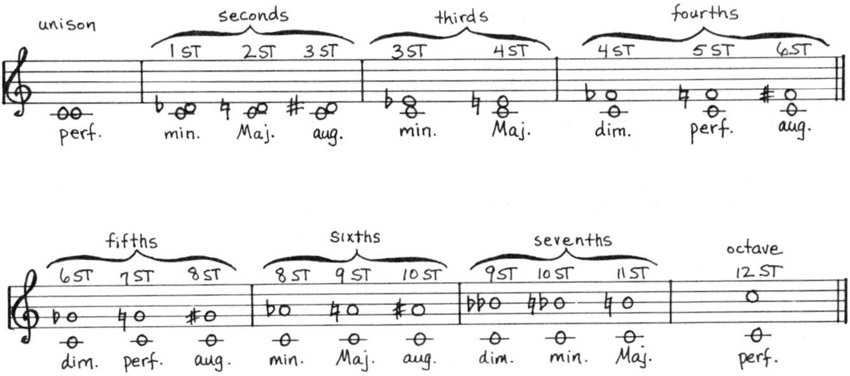

Commonly used musical intervals include seconds, thirds, fourths, fifths, sixths and sevenths of various sizes. Example 12 illustrates how these intervals appear on the staff, their names and their "measurement" in terms of semitones. The natural sign (♮) simply cancels the previous accidental—whether it be a sharp or a flat.

In other words, the interval of a minor third (m3 or −3) is *always* equal to three semitones; the interval of a perfect fifth (P5) is *always* equal to seven semitones; the interval of a major sixth (M6 or +6) is *always* equal to nine semitones, and so on.

The pitches in the major and minor scales are related in still other ways than the mere measurement of intervals. Perhaps the best way to illustrate these other relationships is to sing or play Example 13.

13. *C Major Scale*

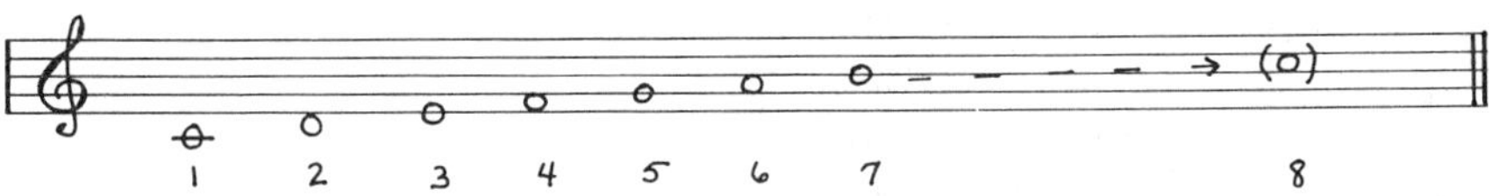

The feeling of incompleteness, or the "pull" towards the completion that the absent eighth tone will supply, is the feeling of *tonality*.

14. *C Major Scale*

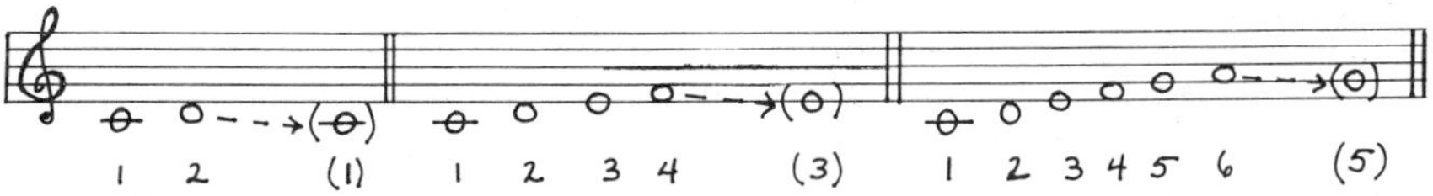

The three segments of the C Major scale in Example 14 illustrate other tendencies or directions that scale steps can indicate. As we play or sing these parts of the scale we feel the pull of scale step 2 to resolve to scale step 1; the pull of scale step 4 to resolve to scale step 3; the pull of scale step 6 to resolve to scale step 5. These are all aspects of the organization of pitch called tonality.

The central pitch in tonality is the first step of the scale—the tonal center or *tonic*. Examples 13 and 14 dealt with segments of the C Major scale and in those examples the pitch, C, has been the tonic—the central pitch in these relationships.

As we have seen, however, we can form a major scale on all available pitches and in each case a different pitch will assume the *function* of the tonic. For example, a major scale formed on G will make us aware of a tonality based on G—G will function as the tonic. Similarly, an E♭ Major scale will make E♭ function as the tonic.

Another way to view this same phenomenon of tonality is to consider the *same* pitch, C, in various scales.

15. Three Major Scales Using the Pitch, C

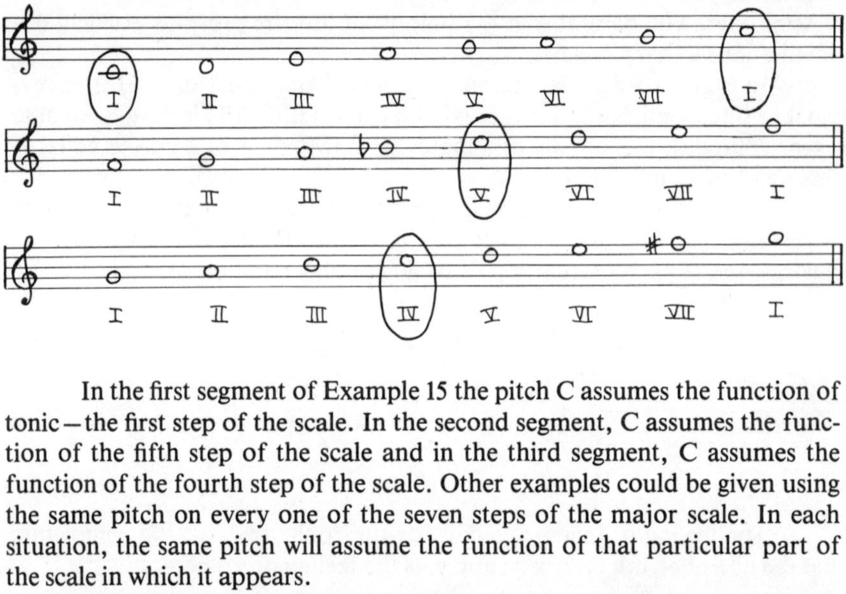

In the first segment of Example 15 the pitch C assumes the function of tonic—the first step of the scale. In the second segment, C assumes the function of the fifth step of the scale and in the third segment, C assumes the function of the fourth step of the scale. Other examples could be given using the same pitch on every one of the seven steps of the major scale. In each situation, the same pitch will assume the function of that particular part of the scale in which it appears.

The quality of tonality which enables the same pitch to serve different functions within the tonal system can be likened to the various roles an individual in our society can assume. The same person can be a father (i.e., can "function" as a father), a son, or a husband.

The tonal system built upon contrasting major and minor scales has attracted Western composers for hundreds of years. For a long time it was the only system in use.

Exercises

1. Below each note, write its letter "name."

2. Place the following pitches on the staves below. (Note: accidentals always are placed *before* the note—and on the same line or space.)

3. Complete the following intervals *above* the given pitch.

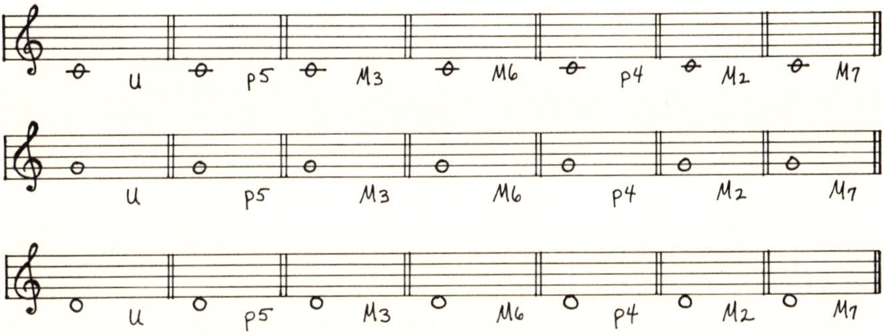

4. Complete the following intervals *below* the given pitch.

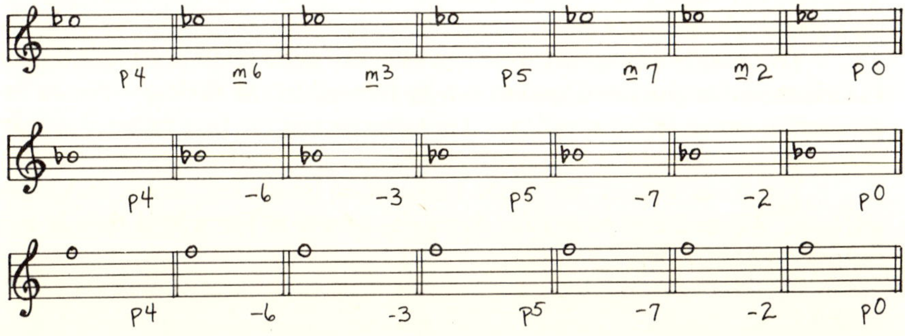

5. Complete the following intervals *above* the given pitch.

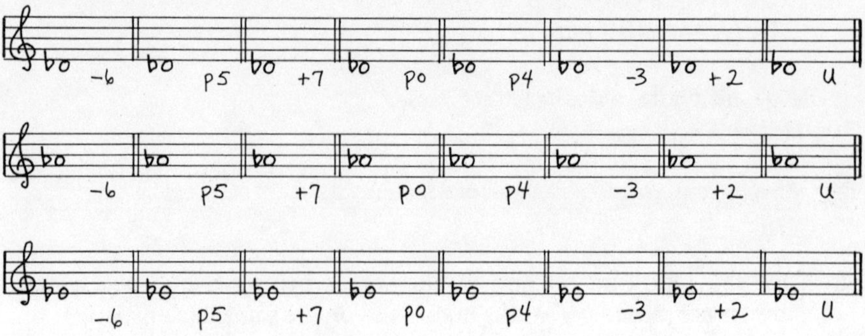

6. Complete the following intervals *below* the given pitch.

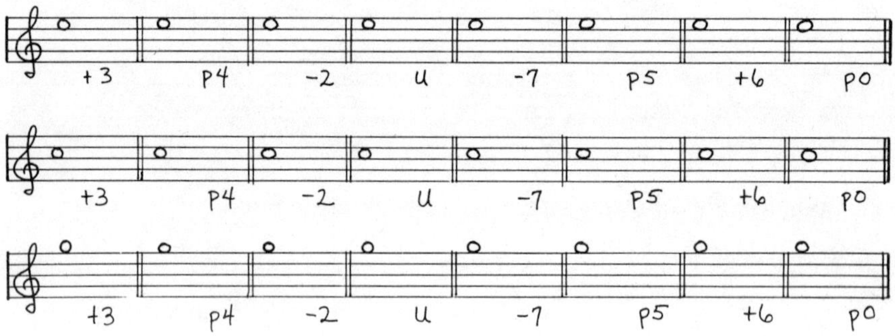

Major Scales and Key Signatures

7. Build major scales on:

F______________________________________

D______________________________________

E♭_____________________________________

A______________________________________

B______________________________________

8. Give the key signature (number of sharps or flats in order) for:

G Major ____________	E+ ____________
B♭ Major____________	F♯+ ____________
C♯M ____________	C+ ____________
A♭M ____________	G♭+____________
D♭M ____________	F+ ____________

9. Give the numerical pattern for the major scale
   Use ⊓ for a whole step
   Use ∧ for a half step

   1 2 3 4 5 6 7 8

10. Define "enharmonic":

11. Give the enharmonic spelling for:
    E♭____________
    C♯____________
    B♭____________

Scales and Intervals

12. Build the following scales:
    A♭ Major____________________________
    e melodic minor____________________________
    f harmonic minor____________________________

13. Build the following intervals (upwards):

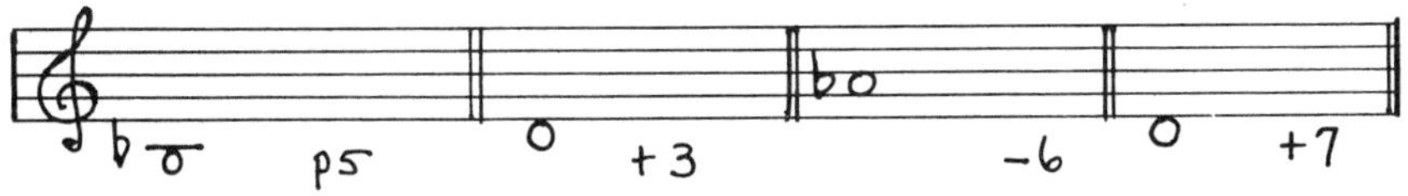

14. Identify the following intervals:

15. Supply the pitch that will produce the desired interval (downwards):

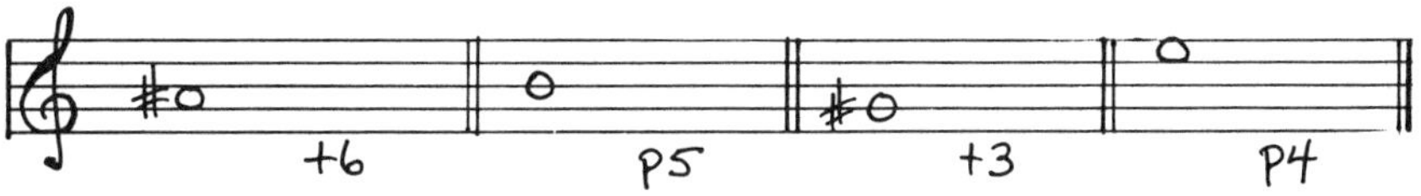

16. Give the correct key signatures.

17. Sing major, natural minor, harmonic minor and melodic minor scales on the same beginning pitch. (Use the piano to guide you.)

18. Write the following major scales and their relative harmonic minor scales on: B♭, D, F, G. (Use key signatures.)

19. Write the following natural minor scales and their relative major scales on: C, C♯, F♯, G. (Use key signatures.)

Listening Assignment

Mozart. *Sonata for Violin and Piano* in F Major, K. 376

Haydn. *Concerto for Trumpet and Orchestra* in E Flat Major

IV. Concepts of Time

Duple and Triple Meter; Simple and Compound Divisions; Commonly Used Time Signatures; Tempo

In a comparison of Western music with music of most other cultures, it is fair to conclude that Westerners have greatly developed harmonic structures while their concepts of both melody and time have been (until very recent years) relatively latent.

The organization of time in Western music is based upon a *beat* or pulse which recurs regularly. Some beats are (or seem) stronger than others and it is this grouping of strong and weak beats that we call *meter*.

The most frequently used meters are: *duple meter*, a combination of a strong and weak beat (e.g. | ı | ı | ı); *triple meter*, a combination of a strong beat and 2 weak beats (e.g. | ı ı | ı ı | ı ı | ı ı), and *quadruple meter*, a combination of a strong beat followed successively by a weak beat, a somewhat stronger beat and a weak beat (e.g. | ı ı ı | ı ı ı | ı ı ı | ı ı ı).

As a mechanical aid in standard notation, each complete unit of a meter is separated from other units into *measures* or *bars* by drawing a single verticle line (*a bar line*) through the staff. Two vertical lines (a double bar) indicate the end of a composition or a section of a composition.

16. A Staff Divided into Measures by Bar Lines

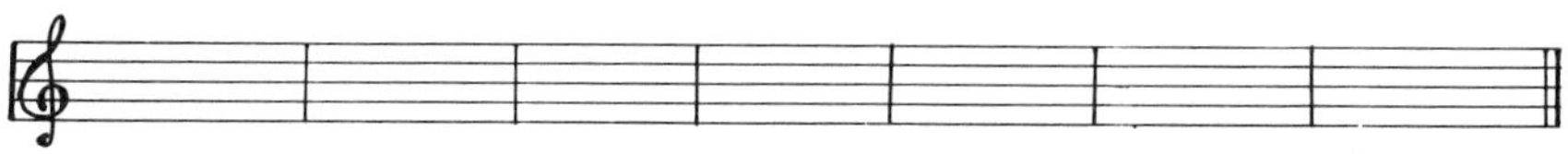

Now let's consider the symbols used in our written language of music to indicate the duration of both sounds (notes) and silence (rests). Example 17 contains the most frequently used note values and rests—and their names.

17. Commonly Used Notes and Rests

The durational symbols in Example 17 are meaningless until we associate them with each other so that we can tell "how long the notes are." Example 18 shows that these notes (and of course rests, too) can be added (or divided) like fractions. There is an exact arithmetical relationship between these symbols. Obviously all note values are relative to each other. A specific time value can only be determined by referring to the speed of the composition—*the tempo.*

18. Notes and Their Common Equivalents

**A dot adds half the value of the note or rest.*

The next step in achieving an understanding of time values in standard notation is to make the connection between note symbols and beats and meter. If we make the quarter note (♩) the symbol equal to one beat and intend to compose in duple meter, each measure would contain two beats—a strong beat and a weak beat—and would appear as shown in Example 19.

19. Duple Meter

20. Duple Meter with Time Signature

21. Another Duple Meter

22. Another Duple Meter with Time Signature

As in the case of key signatures and pitch values, notation uses a shorthand system for presenting or defining time values at the beginning of the composition through *time signatures*. The time signature depends upon the note symbol equal to the beat and the number of beats in the measure. Example 19 indicates that a quarter note equals a beat and there are two beats in the measure. The time signature for this situation is $\frac{2}{4}$ as illustrated in Example 20. Two points seem important here: the $\frac{2}{4}$ time signature is simply a symbol which "labels" the note values and meter used in the composition, and as a "learning crutch" it might be helpful to associate the $\frac{2}{4}$ symbol with "two beats in a measure and a quarter note equals a beat."

Examples 21 and 22 are also in duple meter. Since the note symbol equal to the beat is now a halfnote—but there are still two beats in the measure—the time signature that "labels" this situation is $\frac{2}{2}$.

Examples 23 and 24 contain segments of familiar compositions written in duple meter. Note the position of both key and time signatures at the beginnings of each example.

Frequently used time signatures for triple meter (see examples 25 and 26) are $\frac{3}{4}$ and $\frac{3}{2}$. The $\frac{3}{4}$ symbol means that there are three beats in a measure

" > " is a symbol for "accent."

23. Yankee Doodle

24. London Bridge

and a quarter note equals a beat. The $\frac{3}{2}$ symbol means that there are three beats in a measure and a half note equals a beat. Well known melodies in triple meter follow in examples 27 and 28.

25. Triple Meter

26. Triple Meter

27. America

28. The Star-Spangled Banner

Quadruple meter symbols such as $\frac{4}{4}$ (sometimes called common time and symbolized "C") and $\frac{4}{2}$ indicate respectively that there are four beats in a measure and a quarter note equals a beat ($\frac{4}{4}$) and there are four beats in a measure and a half note equals a beat ($\frac{4}{2}$). Examples 29, 30 and 31 are all written in quadruple meter.

29. Quadruple Meter

30. Swanee River

31. Auld Lang Syne

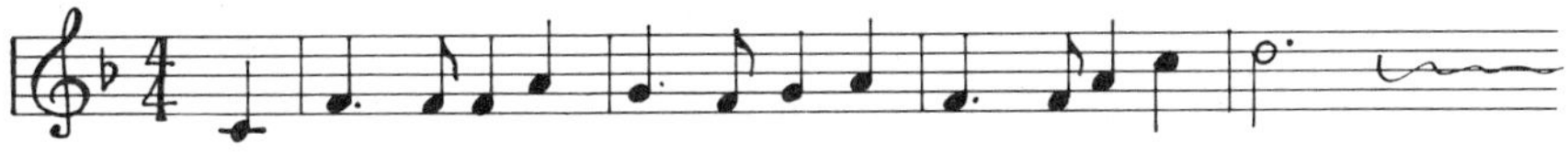

So far in our discussion of the organization of time we have considered the number of beats in a measure and the note values equal to a beat. We have not yet taken into account the division of the individual beat. All the previous examples (19 through 31) with time signatures of $\frac{2}{4}$, $\frac{2}{2}$, $\frac{3}{4}$, $\frac{3}{2}$, $\frac{4}{4}$, or $\frac{4}{2}$ all indicate the number of quarter notes or half notes in a measure *and* each of these symbols is divisible by two. In others words, ♩ = ♫ or 𝅗𝅥 = ♩♩ (see Example 18). The complete description of these previously illustrated meters is duple-simple meter (not duple meter), triple-simple meter (not triple meter) and quadruple-simple meter (not quadruple meter). In each case, "simple" indicates the division of the individual quarter note or half note into two's or multiples of two.

32. When Johnny Comes Marching Home Again

33. Drink to Me Only with Thine Eyes

Examples 32 and 33 contain the beginning phrases from familiar folk songs whose melodies clearly indicate two beats in each measure. The melodies also indicate that each beat is divisible by three. The notation shows that a dotted quarter note is equal to one beat (see Example 18). The missing time signature that describes this meter is $\frac{6}{8}$. The meter is called "duple-compound." Duple-compound meter always specifies music which has two beats in a measure with each beat divisible by three. It should be stated that in compound meter the pulse is *always represented by a dotted note*!

*A "tie" (♩. ‿ ♩) links two notes of the same pitch in order to extend the duration of the sound.

Example 34

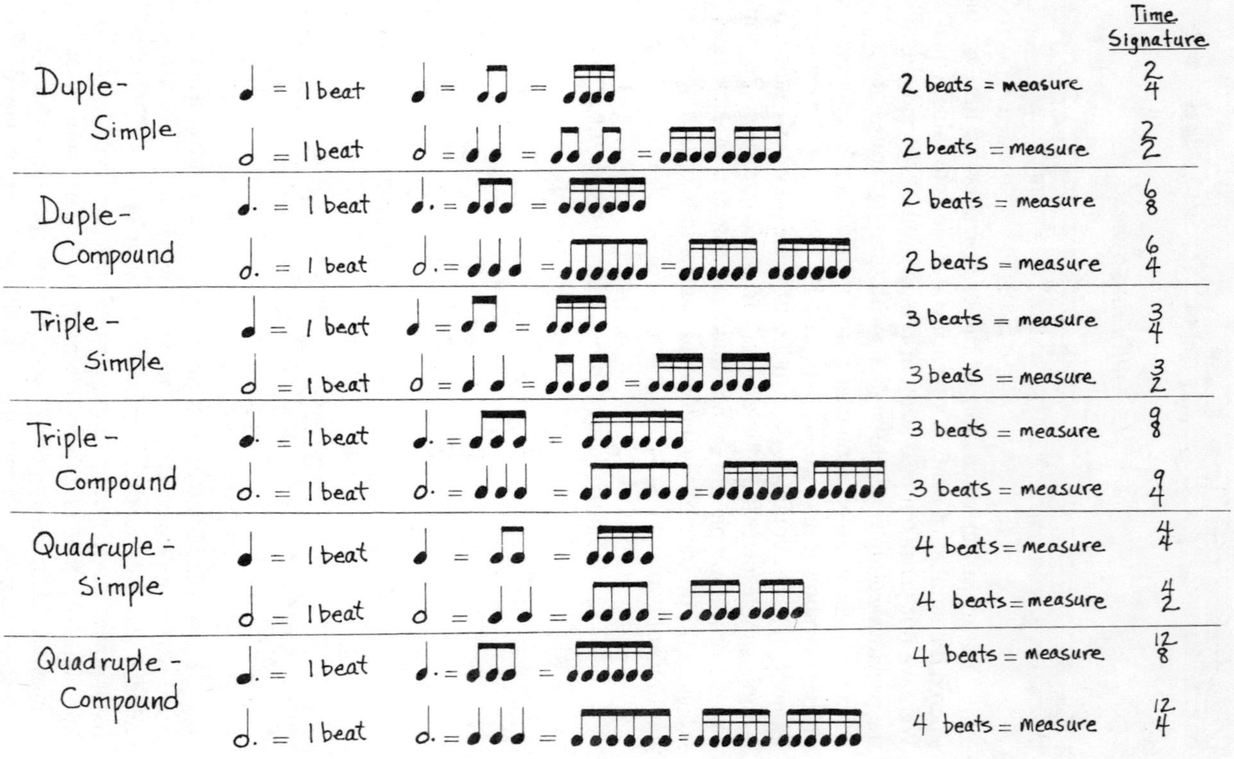
Time Signature
Duple-Simple
= 1 beat
2 beats = measure
2/4
= 1 beat
2 beats = measure
2/2
Duple-Compound
= 1 beat
2 beats = measure
6/8
= 1 beat
2 beats = measure
6/4
Triple-Simple
= 1 beat
3 beats = measure
3/4
= 1 beat
3 beats = measure
3/2
Triple-Compound
= 1 beat
3 beats = measure
9/8
= 1 beat
3 beats = measure
9/4
Quadruple-Simple
= 1 beat
4 beats = measure
4/4
= 1 beat
4 beats = measure
4/2
Quadruple-Compound
= 1 beat
4 beats = measure
12/8
= 1 beat
4 beats = measure
12/4

Example 35

Duple
Triple
Quadruple
Simple
= 1 beat
or
= 1 beat
2 beats = measure, 2/4 or 2/2
3 beats = measure, 3/4 or 3/2
4 beats = measure, 4/4 or 4/2
Duple
Triple
Quadruple
Compound
= 1 beat
or
= 1 beat
2 beats = measure, 6/8 or 6/4
3 beats = measure, 9/8 or 9/4
4 beats = measure, 12/8 or 12/4

The charts in examples 34, 35 and 36 are helpful in clarifying the various factors that make up the most frequently used meters in Western music—and the time signatures that "announce" them. Further division of the beat in either simple or compound meter is referred to a "sub-division" (i.e. $\frac{2}{4}$ ♩ = ♫ = ♬♬ or $\frac{6}{8}$ ♩. = ♪♪♪ = ♬♬♬).

Example 36

Usual Simple Time Signatures		*Usual Compound Time Signatures*	
$\frac{2}{4}$	$\frac{2}{2}$	$\frac{6}{8}$	$\frac{6}{4}$
$\frac{3}{4}$	$\frac{3}{2}$	$\frac{9}{8}$	$\frac{9}{4}$
$\frac{4}{4}$	$\frac{4}{2}$	$\frac{12}{8}$	$\frac{12}{4}$

The previous three examples present the same information in different ways. Simply put, the organization of time in Western music depends upon the note symbol equal to a beat, the division of this symbol into either two's or three's, and the number of such symbols in a measure.

The time signatures we use are merely symbols that represent the preceding information and should be perceived in the same way we understand other familiar symbols—$; H^2O; ©; £, etc.

Thousands of compositions have been written by hundreds of Western composers, all using this limited range of time-values. It seems that in our desire to develop our harmonic resources we purposely neglected comparable developments in the organization of time.

Only one further aspect of time in music need be considered here—*tempo*, the speed at which the beat occurs. Tempo is indicated by the composer at the beginning of the composition and elsewhere either by the customary Italian terminology (see listing below) or English equivalents. Occasionally a metronome marking is used along with verbal instructions for more exactness.*

The tempo markings that follow suggest the character or mood of the composition as well as the speed of the recurring beats.

This chapter has discussed the beat, meter and tempo as aspects of the organization of time in Western music. All of these aspects are part of what we call rhythm. Rhythm (from the Greek for "flow") is all of the things pointed out here—and more. It is the duration of sounds and silences, the regularity (or irregularity) of the pulse, the dynamic contrast which creates meter, the subtle nuances added by the performer, and the overall "flow" of

**The metronome is a simple machine producing a beat, usually set in terms of pulses per minute. For example, a metronome marking (sometimes, "M.M.") of "♩ = 120" means the tempo of the quarter note is 120 per minute.*

Common Terminology for Tempo

Italian	*English*
Largo	Very slow
Adagio	Slow
Lento	Slow
Andante	Walking pace
Moderato	Moderate
Allegretto	Moderately fast
Allegro	Joyful
Vivace	Fast

musical expression. I know of no adequate verbal description of this dimension of music. One may imagine, however, a mechanical metrical reading of a poem (*any* poem) compared to a reading of the same poem by a knowledgeable, skillful, talented actor. The first result will produce the meter of the poem, the second result will contain the rhythm that the *meaning* of the words signify.

Exercises

1. If $\frac{2}{4}$ is the time signature, ______ is the note equal to 1 beat
   If $\frac{4}{4}$ is the time signature, ______ is the note equal to 1 beat
   If $\frac{9}{8}$ is the time signature, ______ is the note equal to 1 beat
   If $\frac{6}{8}$ is the time signature, ______ is the note equal to 1 beat

2. If $\frac{3}{4}$ is the time signature, there are ______ beats in each measure
   If $\frac{6}{8}$ is the time signature, there are ______ beats in each measure
   If $\frac{12}{4}$ is the time signature, there are ______ beats in each measure
   If $\frac{12}{8}$ is the time signature, there are ______ beats in each measure

3. If $\frac{2}{4}$ is the time signature, each beat is divided into ______ eighth notes
   If $\frac{9}{8}$ is the time signature, each beat is divided into ______ eighth notes
   If $\frac{3}{8}$ is the time signature, each beat is divided into ______ eighth notes
   If $\frac{5}{4}$ is the time signature, each beat is divided into ______ eighth notes

4. $\frac{6}{8}$ is a time signature indicating ______ ______ meter
   $\frac{3}{4}$ is a time signature indicating ______ ______ meter

$\frac{9}{8}$ is a time signature indicating ______ ______ meter
$\frac{3}{2}$ is a time signature indicating ______ ______ meter

5. Exercises to be sung to experience time organization and pitch relationships. Use the piano to "check" pitches and always beat time with your foot or a pencil. Use as many other musical examples as time allows from any collection of folk songs.

Key of C Major

Key of A Major

Key of A♭ Major

Key of E♭ Major

Key of G Major

Key of E Major

Key of E♭ Major

Wiegenlied (Brahms)

Key of C Major

Liebestraum (Liszt)

6. Common Terms for Dynamic Levels

pp	=	pianissimo	=	very softly
p	=	piano	=	softly
mp	=	mezzo piano	=	moderately softly
mf	=	mezzo forte	=	moderately loudly
f	=	forte	=	forte
ff	=	fortissimo	=	very loudly

Listening Assignment

Bach. *Brandenburg Concerto* no. 2 in F Major

Chopin. *Mazurka* in c♯ minor, op. 6, no. 2

Ravel. *Bolero*

V. Discussion of Triads

Types; Functions; Theory of Inversion

As noted earlier, the music of Western culture tends to emphasize the harmonic (that is, what may be called the "vertical") aspects of sound and perhaps the most basic harmonic unit is the triad. As its name implies, a triad contains three different pitches arranged in a "ladder of thirds" and can be built on each step of major and minor scales.

Example 37

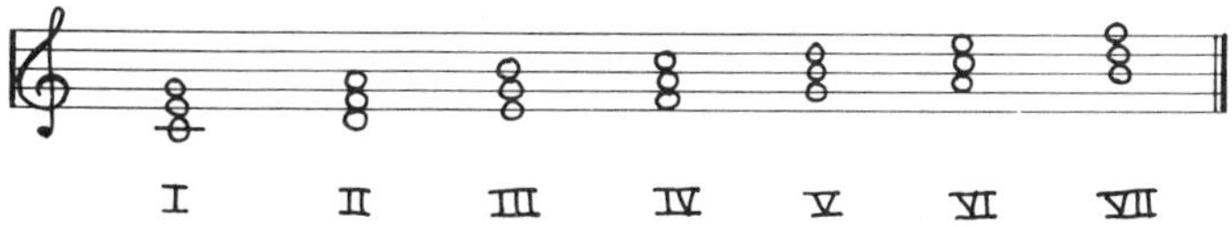

The triads built on the degrees of any major scale (Example 37) will produce variously constructed triads. For example, the triads built on I, IV and V of any major scale will produce a sonority made up of a major third and a perfect fifth (counting from the lowest pitch). This is by definition a major triad. The sonorities produced on II, III and VI contain a minor third and a perfect fifth—by definition, a minor triad. The sonority produced by building a triad on VII contains a minor third and a diminished fifth—by definition, a diminished triad. Note that all triads have been produced by constructing a ladder of thirds upwards using only those pitches found in that particular major scale.

It is interesting to observe that fewer than half of the triads built on all steps of a major scale result in major triads and yet the Western ear easily accepts the major mode when exposed to these various sonorities. Perhaps an important reason for this is the fact that the triads built on the tonal degrees of the scale—I, IV and V—are all major.

Example 38

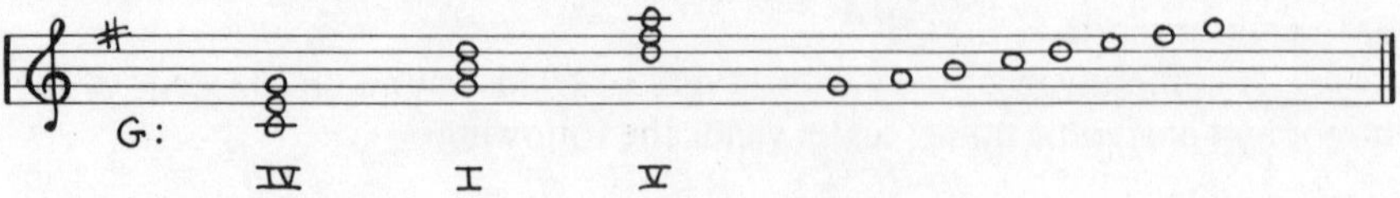

The above example in the key of G Major illustrates that major triads built a perfect fifth above and below any given major triad will produce all the pitches that form the elements of a major scale.

This may be an important reason for building triads in the minor mode and emphasizing the harmonic minor scale.

Example 39

By building minor triads on I and IV but keeping the major triad on V, all the degrees of the harmonic minor scale are produced. These chords seem to identify the minor mode to the Western ear and at the same time supply the leading tone (seventh step of the scale raised—the middle voice of the V triad) for ready access to the tonic.

Example 40

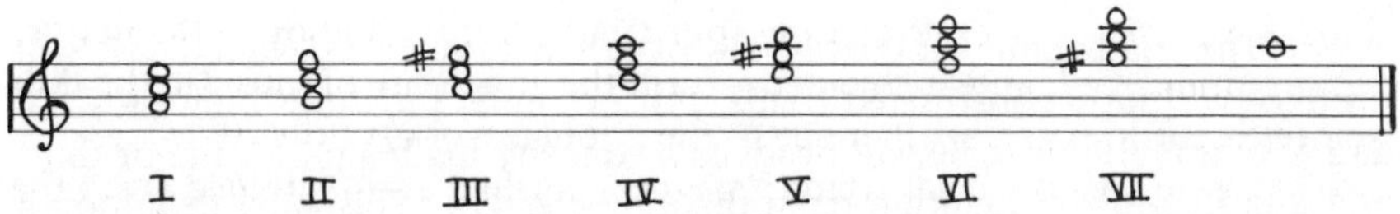

The triads built on the steps of any harmonic minor scale (Example 40) produce variously constructed triads—and, in most cases, different sonorities from those found in the major scale. The triads built on I and IV are minor triads because they are composed of a minor third and a perfect fifth. The triads built on V and VI are major triads because they are composed of a major third and a perfect fifth. The triads built on II and VII are composed of a minor triad and a diminished fifth—by definition a diminished triad. Finally the III triad is composed of a major third and an augmented fifth—by definition an augmented triad. It is important to realize that all of these triads have been constructed from the lowest to the highest pitch in each case.

As noted above, although less than half the triads formed from the major scale are major triads, the Western ear easily recognizes major mode. Similarly, only two of a possible seven triads formed from the harmonic minor scale are minor triads and again the Western ear accepts this material as the minor mode.

A comparison of the various types of triads found on the steps of the major and harmonic minor scales yields the following:

Types of Triads Formed on Steps of Major and Harmonic Minor Scales

I	*II*	*III*	*IV*	*V*	*VI*	*VII*
Major	minor	minor	Major	Major	minor	diminished
minor	diminished	augmented	minor	Major	Major	diminished

The major triad can now be associated with triads built on I, IV and V in the major mode as well as triads built on V and VI in the harmonic minor mode. Likewise, the minor triad can be associated with triads built on II, III and VI in the major mode and I and IV in the harmonic minor mode. In other words, the sonority we define as a major triad built on any given pitch can function as I (tonic) in one major scale, IV (subdominant) in another major scale, V (dominant) in still another major or harmonic minor scale and VI (submediant) in a harmonic minor scale. For example, the C Major triad can function as a tonic triad in C Major, a subdominant triad in G Major, a dominant triad in either F Major or f harmonic minor and a submediant triad in e harmonic minor. This concept of various functions for a given sonority is extremely useful in the theory of music and has important ramifications in many areas of the discipline.

Although other triadic sounds are possible (through use of the diminished third, for example) the four triads discussed above – the major, minor, diminished, and augmented – form the great bulk of music in the 18th and 19th centuries and are in many of the popular works of the 20th.

Up to this point all triads have been spelled and identified from the bottom rung of a ladder of thirds. Unfortunately, this was not always true and a debt is owed to Jean Philippe Rameau (1683–1764) for his so-called "theory of inversion" which clarified this practice. In other words, a triad consisting of C, E and G will always be identified as a C Major triad no matter how these tones are distributed vertically.

Example 41

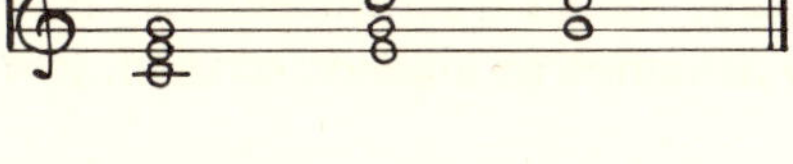

The triads in Example 41 are all identified as C Major triads—not a triad built on C, another built on E and still another built on G. In this case the C is known as the *root* or *fundamental* of the triad, the E and G are identified respectively as the *third* and *fifth* of the triad. When the E is the lowest pitch produced, the sonority is said to be a first inversion of a C Major triad. When the G is the lowest pitch produced, the sonority is known as a second inversion of the C Major triad. This terminology enables the sonority to keep its root or "identity" no matter how the individual parts of the triad are distributed in pitch range.

Exercises

1. Identify aurally major, minor, diminished and augmented triads.
2. Sing the triads on each step of the major and harmonic minor scale.
3. How can a major triad built on F be used in major and harmonic minor scales (i.e. I in F Major, etc.)?
4. How can a minor triad on d be used in major and harmonic minor scales?
5. How can a diminished triad on e be used?
6. How can an augmented triad on C be used?

Scales and Intervals

7. Build the following scales:

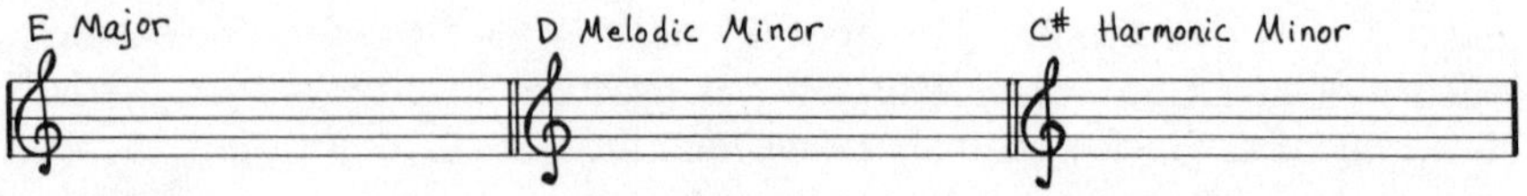

8. Build the following intervals upwards:

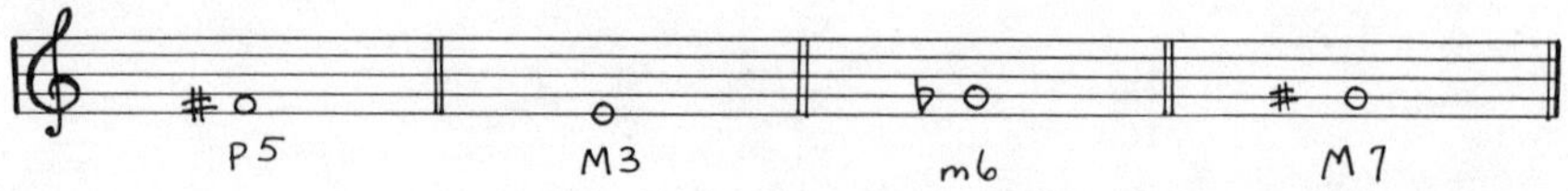

9. Identify the following intervals:

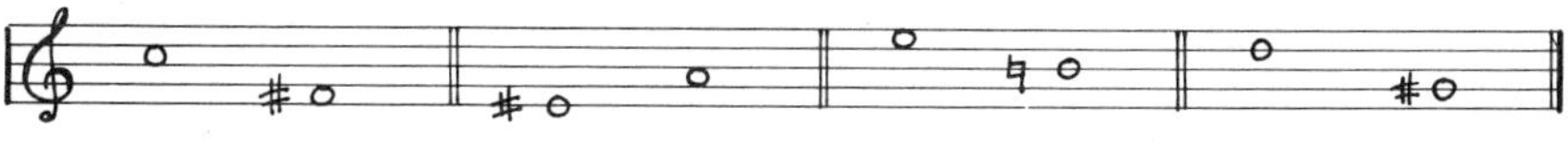

10. Supply the pitch which will produce the desired interval downwards:

11. Give the correct key signatures:

12. Build the following scales — with key signatures:

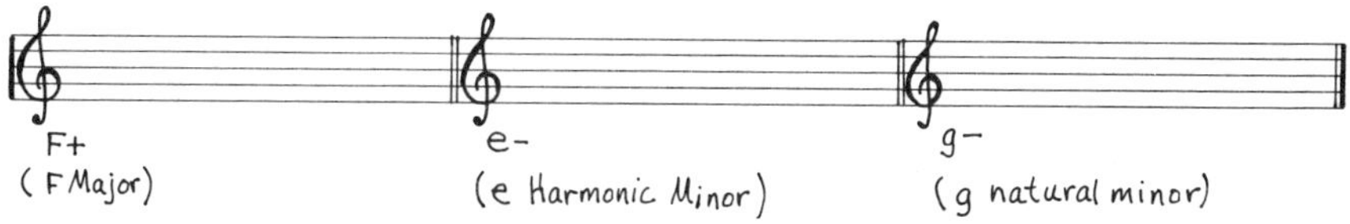

13. Give the correct key signatures:

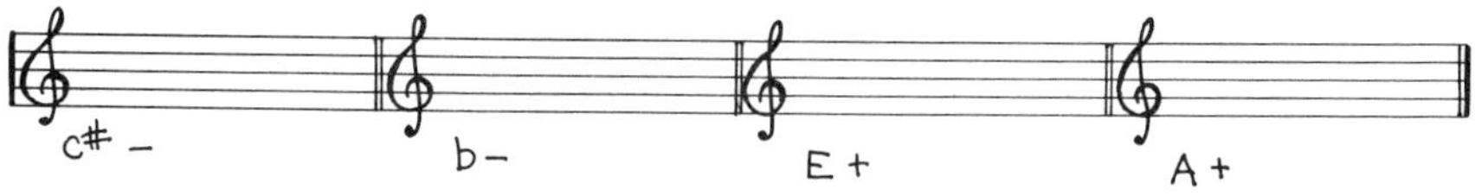

14. Identify the following intervals:

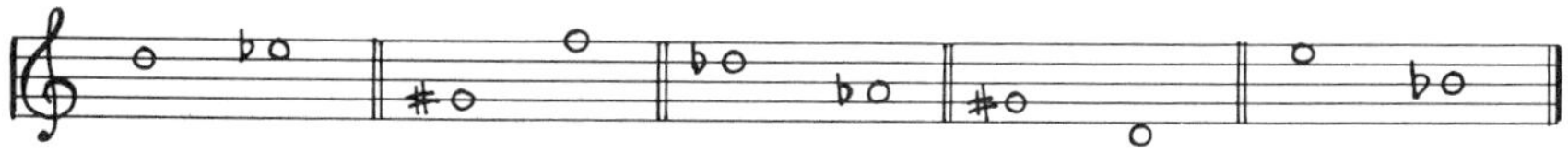

15. Triad Spellings:

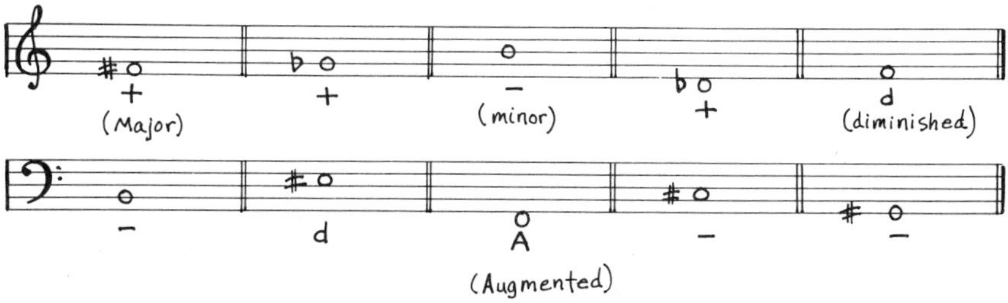

16. Key signatures:

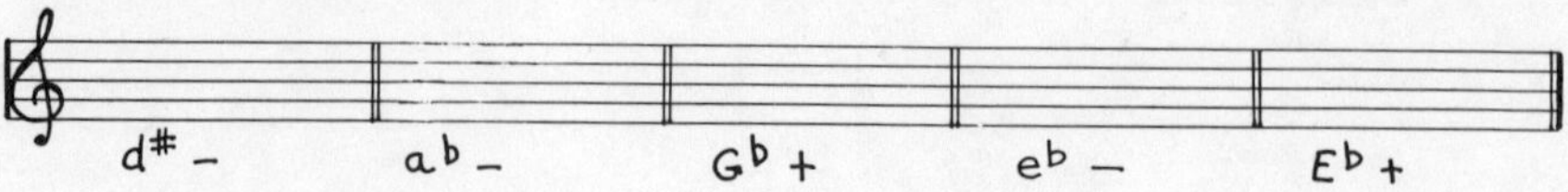

17. Intervals (upwards):

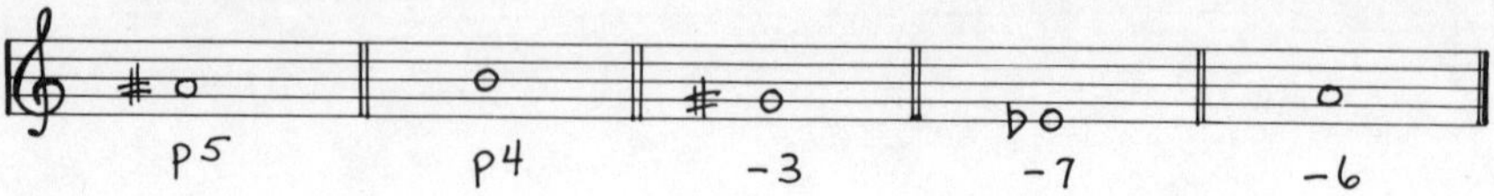

Triads

18. Spell a major triad with:

B as third____________
G♯ as root____________
F♯ as fifth____________

19. Spell a minor triad with:

E♭ as fifth____________
F♯ as third____________
A♯ as root____________

20. Triads in a key:

IV in e minor__________
VI in D Major__________
II in A Major__________

21. Key signatures:

D♭ Major____________
f minor____________
g ♯ minor____________

Scales

22. Major scale on:

G♭____________________________
E____________________________
B____________________________

23. Harmonic minor scale on:

G____________________________
D____________________________
A♭____________________________

Listening Assignment

Mozart. *Symphony no. 23* in D Major, K. 181

Haydn. *String Quartet*, op. 76, no. 1

VI. The Theory of the Progression of Chords

Fundamental Bass; Classification of Chords; Establishing Tonality

Once the concept of the "theory of inversion" is understood and a triad can be recognized no matter which pitch is the lowest sounding, we then need to consider how a triad (any triad) moves or progresses to another. The principles of this logical "right-sounding" progression of harmonic sounds were first codified by the same Jean Philippe Rameau who proposed the theory of inversion in the 18th century.

Rameau began the development of his theory by a careful analysis of music by his contemporaries in the mid 18th century. By creating another staff below an existing composition, he was able to notate the roots of each chord. This series of roots of chords was called the *fundamental bass* and enabled Rameau to chart the intervallic distance from one root to another.

Example 42 illustrates the analysis necessary to develop the fundamental bass. Note that the fundamental bass line is simply a series of roots of chords and does not necessarily coincide with the original musical bass line of J.S. Bach.

Briefly stated, Rameau's theory of the progression of chords, based upon extensive analysis of actual music (not theoretical examples), tells us that the best (i.e., most frequent) progression of roots of chords is down a perfect fifth (or up a perfect fourth—which is the same thing).

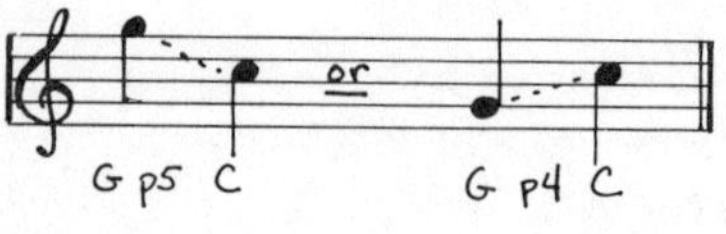

42. Chorale: Lobt Gott, ihr Christen allgugleich (Bach)

Another way to consider the same concept would be to analyze a composition whose central pitch (or point of rest, or finality) is a C Major triad—the tonic. Our theory of the progression of chords tells us that the chord most frequently preceeding a C triad would be a chord built upon G (the root movement would be down a perfect fifth—or up a perfect fourth). Furthermore, the chord preceding the G chord would be one built upon D—again a movement of a descending perfect fifth.

43. Progression of Chords with a Tonic of C Major

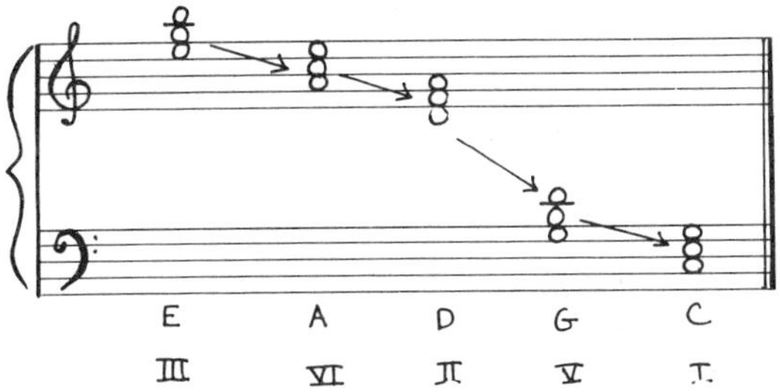

The progression of chords in Example 43 all move by descending P5 illustrating this frequent intervallic relationship. Each chord is identified by a roman numeral based upon the tonic of C (C = I). This means that in theory as well as practice our music is built upon the principle that a V chord will most frequently progress to I; that a II chord will most frequently progress to V; that a VI will progress to II–V–I, etc.

But our seven note scale is incomplete—we still need to account for IV and VII.

Example 44 is an example of a complete progression of chords with a C Major tonic. In both theory and practice both the V and VII chords most frequently progress to the tonic. Note that the V and VII chords contain two pitches in common—and one of these is the leading tone (the seventh step of the scale) whose strong tendency towards the tonic was noted in Chapter III.

44. Progression of Chords with a Tonic of C Major

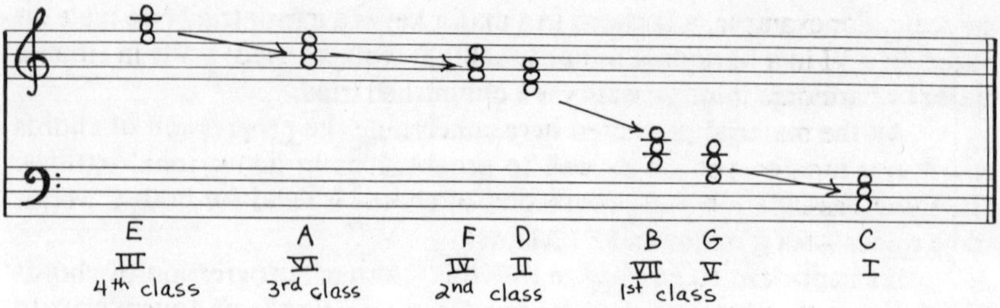

By definition the V and VII chords that normally progress to the tonic are called *first class chords.*

In both theory and practice the II and IV chords most frequently progress to first class chords. Note again that these chords contain two pitches in common. By definition the II and IV chords that usually progress to first class chords, are called *second class chords*. By the same logic, the VI chord is a *third class chord* and the III chord is a *fourth class chord.*

The importance of the interval of the perfect fifth in Western music is highly evident in the theory (and practice) of our progression of chords. It is interesting to note again the parallel between this cultural value and the physical characteristics of sound—the P5 is the intervallic distance between the second and third partials of the harmonic series (see Chapter II) and is second in accoustical importance only to the basic interval of the octave.

The movement of one chord to another or from one classification of chords to another within the framework of this theory of the progression of chords establishes tonality as surely as would following the tendencies of individual pitches. The "vertical" and "horizontal" aspects of music work together to produce the feeling of tonality.

Chords as well as individual pitches can assume different functions depending upon position within the scale or key center. For example, a C Major triad can be I in the key of C Major. The same C Major triad can also be IV in the key of G Major of V in the key of F Major. Example 45 illustrates this change in function or usage.

45. Three Major Scales Using the C Major Triad

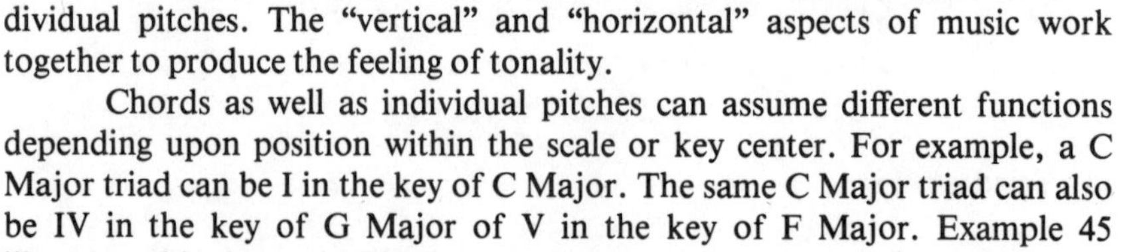

Note the similarity between Example 15 (Chapter III) in which a single pitch assumes various functions depending upon its position in the scale and Example 45 above in which a complete triad can assume various functions based upon the same criterion.

Of course, in considering the various functions a triad can assume, it is important to recognize the *type* of triad as well as its possible position in the scale. For example, a II chord in a major key is a minor triad (see table on page 37); a VI in a harmonic minor tonality is a major triad; a VII in either a major or harmonic minor tonality is a diminished triad.

All the material presented here concerning the progression of chords in a major tonality pertain as well to progressions in minor tonal settings. The same classification and progression of chords is valid for both C Major and e minor – for g minor and E♭ Major.

It's important to emphasize that this "normal" progression of chords simply means that *most of the time* regular progression from fourth class to third class to second class to first class to tonic holds true for the great bulk of music composed in the 17th, 18th, 19th and a sizeable portion of the 20th centuries. To stray too far from these principles would do serious harm to tonality. Conversely, too strict an observance of this procedure would become terribly boring in a very short time.

If this were a how-to-cook book it would be highly desirable to taste the mixture of ingredients. Instead, this is a how-to-make-music book and it is highly desirable (even necessary) to listen to the musical examples. The elusive nuances of the progression of chords can be completely lost if this book is merely read. The proof of the music is in the hearing!

Exercises

1. Triad spelling:

major on G♭ ____________ minor on C♯ ____________
major on F♯ ____________ diminished on G♭ ____________
minor on D♭ ____________ augmented on G ____________
major on B ____________ minor on B♭ ____________
diminished on F♯ ____________ minor on A♭ ____________

2. Key signatures:

d♭ minor ____________ d♭ minor ____________
a♯ minor ____________ A Major ____________
B Major ____________

3. Intervals:

perfect fifth on G♯__________ minor seventh on D♭ ____________
perfect fourth on A ________ minor sixth on G ______________
minor third on F♯ _________

4. Scales:

C♯ is the sixth degree of the ______ major scale
third degree of the ______ minor scale
fifth degree of the ______ major scale
seventh degree of the ______ harmonic minor scale
fifth degree of the ______ minor scale

5. Triads:

A is the third of the ______ minor triad
fifth of the ______ diminished triad
third of the ______ augmented triad
fifth of the ______ major triad
third of the ______ major triad

6. Triads in a key:

IV in E Major ______
V in d harmonic minor ______
VII in f♯ harmonic minor ______
III in B♭ Major ______
II in C♭ Major ______

7. Key signatures:

g♯ minor _________
a♭ minor _________
D Major _________
E♭ Major _________
E Major _________

8. Intervals (identify):

D down to B♭ ___________
A♭ down to G ___________
B down to G♯ ___________
D down to G♯ ___________
B♭ down to E ___________

9. Spell a major triad on:

G♯ ______________
A♭ ______________
B♭ ______________
F♯ ______________
D♭ ______________

10. Spell a minor triad on:

B ______________
C♯ ______________
A♯ ______________
G♭ ______________
F♯ ______________

11. Build the following intervals:

minor second on B♭ ____________ minor third on E♭ ____________
major second on F♯ ____________ dim. fifth on D♭ ____________

12. Key signatures:

D Major ____________ e minor ____________
F♯ Major ____________ d minor ____________
D♭ Major ____________ f minor ____________
C♭ Major ____________ c minor ____________
A Major ____________ c♯ minor ____________

13. Give the relative minor to:

G Major ____________
F Major ____________
E♭ Major ____________
B Major ____________
C♯ Major ____________

14. Give the relative major to:

f♯ minor ____________
d♯ minor ____________
c♯ minor ____________
g minor ____________
b minor ____________

15. Build a major scale on:

A♭ ________________
B ________________

16. Build a pure minor scale on:

D ________________
F♯ ________________

17. Build a harmonic minor scale on:

F ________________
B ________________

18. Build a melodic minor scale on:

E ________________
B♭ ________________

19. Spell:

Major scale on B ______________________
Pure minor scale on F♯ ______________________
Harmonic minor scale on E♭ ______________________
Melodic minor (ascending) on C♯ ______________________

20. Key signatures:

g minor ____________ F♯ Major ____________
f minor ____________ a♭ minor ____________
D♭ Major ____________ A Major ____________

21. Intervals:

major seventh on F♯ ________
minor sixth on E♭ ________
aug. fourth on C♭ ________
major third on D♯ ________
dim. fifth on A♯ ________

22. Triads:

major on F♯ ________
minor on E♭ ________
dim. on G♯ ________
aug. on D♭ ________
major on A♯ ________
minor with E as third ________

23. Triads in a key:

V in d minor ________
IV in E Major ________
VII in B Major ________
III in E Major ________
VI in b minor ________

24. Spell a major triad with

C♯ as third ________
A♯ as root ________
G♯ as fifth ________

25. Spell a minor triad with

F as fifth ________
G♯ as third ________
B as root ________

26. Triads in a key:

IV in d minor ________
VI in B♭ Major ________
II in E Major ________

27. Key signatures:

B Major ________
c♯ minor ________
b♭ minor ________

Scales

28. Major scale on

F♯ ________________
A♭ ________________
D♭ ________________

29. Harmonic minor scale on

B ________________
E ________________
A♯ ________________

30. Triad 1 is: I in what major key?
IV in what major key?
V in what major or minor key?
VI in what minor key?
Triad 2 is: III in what minor key?
Triad 3 is: II in what minor key?
VII in what major key?
Triad 4 is: I in what minor key?
II in what major key?
III in what major key?
IV in what minor key?
VI in what major key?

31. In what M and m keys and upon what scale steps are each of the following triads to be found? (List under each chord.)

32. Analysis of chord progressions:

Chorale: O Welt, sieh hier dein Leben (Bach)

Chorale: Was, fürchtst du, Feind Herodes, sehr (Bach)

33. Analysis: Place under each chord the roman numeral identification of each chord. What is the key center?

Chorale: Wir Christenleut (Bach)

34. Analysis: As above. Last 2 phrases only.

Chorale: O Gott, du frommer Gott (Bach)

35. In the following examples, indicate: key; chord choice (roman numeral) classification.

Sonata for Piano, K. 281 (Mozart)

Sonata for Piano, no. 16 (Haydn)

Sonata for Violin and Piano, op. 24 (Beethoven)

36. Continue using folk song collections to experience tonal concepts and time organization. Beat time with your foot or a pencil and "check" pitches with piano.

Listening Assignment

Haydn. *Symphony no. 101 in D Major*

Mozart. *Quintet for Clarinet and Strings in A Major, K. 581*

Beethoven. *Symphony no. 8 in F Major, op. 93*

Composition

C Major; $\frac{3}{4}$ time; 4 measures

I | IV | V | I ||

Composition should be "song-like" and may be sung or played upon an orchestral instrument. The accompaniment should be "in the left hand"—in any style—(i.e., block chords [see Bach examples], arpeggiated [see Beethoven example], etc.). Guitars, orchestral instruments and voices can and should be used (if available) as well as piano. Ideally, all compositions should be performed by the instructor and/or the students during the same class period. Individuality is certain to be pronounced and this will prompt comments and suggestions from both instructor and students about melody, meter, phrasing and performance practice.

VII. Cadences and Other Aspects of Rhythm and Meter

A phrase in music is often compared to a sentence in our written language. And, as is true of our sentence structure, these phrases require various kinds of "endings." Phrase endings—called cadences—can carry the finality of a period. Other cadences can be likened to a sentence requiring a comma, a semicolon or a colon.

Example 46

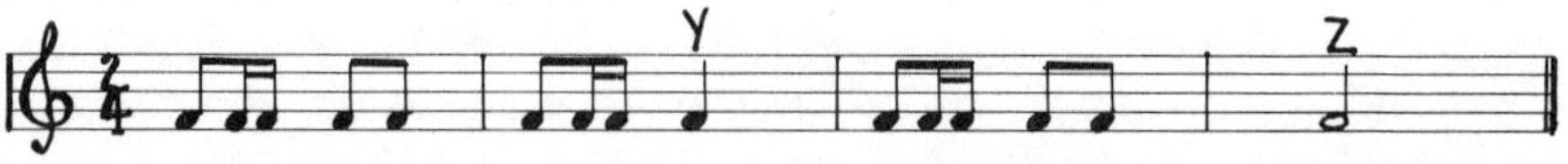

Meter can by itself establish a feeling for cadence. Example 46 illustrates a simple drum beat which indicates what could be a partial cadence at "y" and a complete cadence at "z." In terms of sentence structure, "y" might be a comma and "z" a period.

47. Twinkle, Twinkle Little Star

Cadences can be even more pronounced when melodic and harmonic components are added to metric structure. Example 47 contains three phrases. Phrases one and three end with a finality that indicates the tonic of the key center ("z")—a resting place. The cadence for the second phrase ("y") is far less final and indicates the dominant—a point which we feel almost begs for "more to come."

By far the most common cadence is the melodic/harmonic progression first class to tonic—and the usual chord choice is V–I rather than VII–I (see Chapter VI). In view of what we know about the progression of chords, this is hardly surprising. The V–I cadence (the *authentic cadence*) brings both melody and harmony to a definite point of rest.

Another less final (and less common) cadence is IV–I. Called a *plagal cadence*, it is familiar to us as the "A-men" concluding many of our religious hymns. Note that this second class to tonic movement "skips" a classification (it is IV–I, not IV–V–I) and tends to produce a more subtle ending than the emphatic V–I authentic cadence.

Other less frequent and less final cadences are the *deceptive cadence* (V–VI) and the *half cadence* (I–V).

48. Cadences

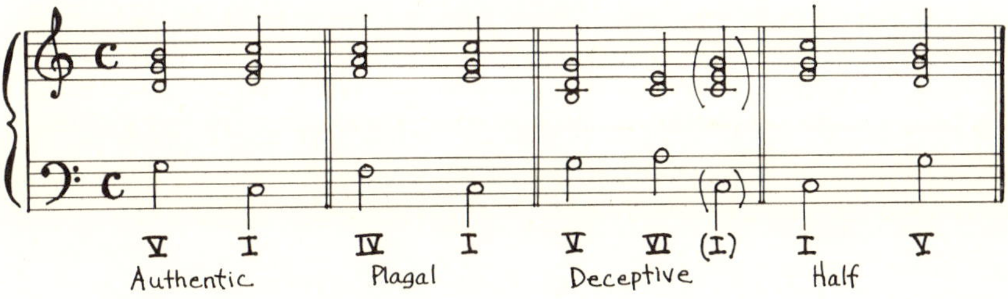

The cadences illustrated in Example 48 are not the only possible endings in Western music, but they are by far the most common. The deceptive cadence resolves to the VI chord, which may seem strange until we compare it to the I chord in parenthesis and note that two of the three chord tones are identical. The half cadence seems to be aptly named. It is not necessary to precede the final chord with I (it might be II or IV). This cadence leaves the listener with an expectation of "waiting for the other shoe to drop."

It now seems appropriate to add more information about meter in

49. Blue Danube Waltz (J. Strauss)

music. The strong interrelationship between tempo and meter can make important changes in our concepts of the rhythmic organization of music.

If the tempo indication in Example 49 is disregarded, the meter would be "triple-simple." That is, there are three beats in each measure, a quarter note is the unit that receives one beat and each beat is divisible by two (♩ = ♫ etc.).

The tempo marking of "Tempo di Valse" changes all of this. The indication now of "waltz time" means that there is one beat in each measure, a dotted half note is the unit that receives one beat and each beat is divisible by three (𝅗𝅥. = ♩♩♩ etc.). In other words, the tempo indication has changed the meter from simple to compound.

50. Peer Gynt Suite no. 1, op. 46 (Grieg)

Example 50 presents another musical theme in which the interpretation of the tempo marking will make a drastic difference in the meter. If, for example, the performer takes "Allegretto pastorale" to mean that the dotted quarter note equals one beat, there are two beats in each measure and the dotted quarter note is divisible by three (♩. = ♪♪♪ etc.), then the meter will be duple-compound. If, on the other hand, the performer "interprets" the same tempo marking to mean that the eighth note equals one beat, there are six beats in each measure and the eighth note is divisible by two (♪ = ♬ etc.), then the meter will be changed from compound to simple.

51. Symphony no. 3, op. 55 (Beethoven)

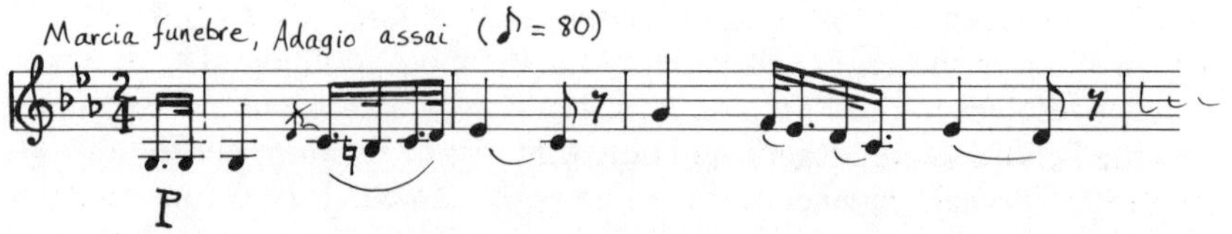

The theme from Beethoven's famous funeral march in Example 51 illustrates how making the eighth note equal to a beat (which the composer clearly indicates) changes the meter from duple to quadruple.

The three preceding examples make clear the necessity of considering both time signature and tempo indication in the performance of music. In other words, the tempo marking can drastically change the concept of the time signature—the same symbol can mean two different things.

Another way of thinking about this same phenomenon is to realize that perhaps Western music has too few symbols to indicate meter. Maybe we need a symbol for $\frac{3}{4}$ at moderate speed and an entirely different symbol for $\frac{3}{4}$ at fast speed!

Exercises

1. The II in E♭ Major (spelled ________) normally progresses to ________ (spelled ________) or ________ (spelled ________).

2. The VI in d minor (spelled ________) normally progresses to ________ (spelled ________) or ________ (spelled ________).

3. The VII in E Major (spelled ________) normally progresses to ________ (spelled ________).

4. The IV in e minor (spelled ________) normally progresses to ________ (spelled ________) or ________ (spelled ________).

5. The V in A Major (spelled ________) in a deceptive cadence normally progresses to ________ (spelled ________).

6. The last chord in a half cadence in b minor is ________ (spelled ________).

7. The III in g minor (spelled ________) normally progresses to ________ (spelled ________).

8. The dominant chord in f♯ minor is ________ (spelled ________).

9. The subdominant chord in c minor is ________ (spelled ________).

10. The leading tone triad in c♯ minor is ________ (spelled ________).

11. Triads in a key (use key signatures):

12. Complete the triad:

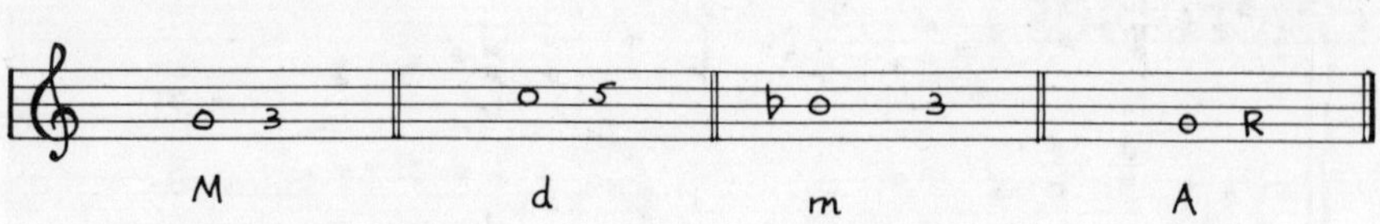

13. In what keys and on what scale steps can the following triads be used? (Use only major and harmonic minor key centers.)

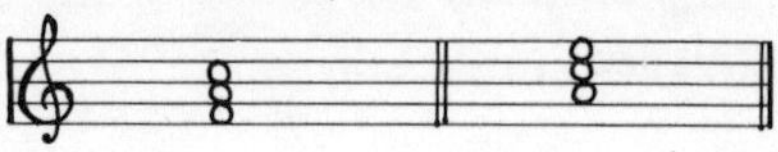

14. Analysis: Indicate the last two chords of each phrase in the given key.

Chorale: O Gott, du frommer Gott (Bach)

15. Analyze these phrases in A Major. What are the cadences?

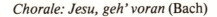

Chorale: Jesu, geh' voran (Bach)

16. Analyze the last three measures. What is the cadence? (The notes for the B♭ clarinet must be lowered a major second to match concert pitch.)

Trio, op. 11 (Beethoven)

17. Make a complete chordal analysis of the following phrases from chorales by J.S. Bach. Indicate the type of cadence in each example.

Chorale: In allen meinen Taten (Bach)

Chorale: Auf meinen lieben Gott (Bach)

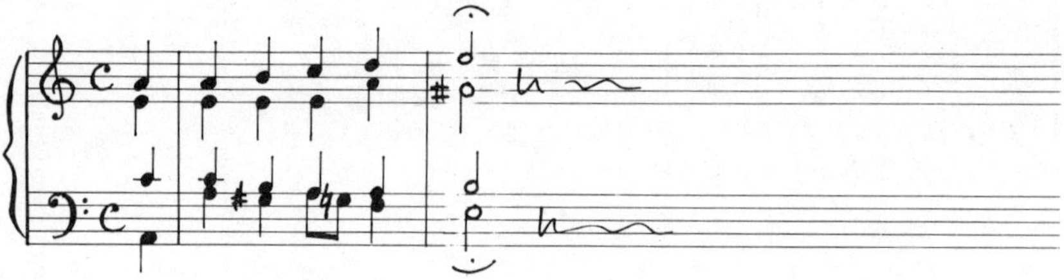

Chorale: Nun danket alle Gott (Bach)

Chorale: Aus meines Herzen Grunde (Bach)

18. Analyze the cadence (the last two measures). What type of cadence? (The notes written for the tenors will sound an octave lower.)

Messiah: Hallelujah Chorus (Handel)

19. Continue using folk song material to practice singing melodic lines. Use the piano to "check" pitches. Use some folk songs to practice reproducing metric structures.

Listening Assignment

Beethoven. *Symphony no. 3* in E Flat Major, op. 55

Grieg. *Peer Gynt Suite no. 1*

J. Strauss. *Blue Danube Waltz*

Composition

G Major; $\frac{6}{8}$ time; 4 measures

I | II | VII | I ||

This should be another "song-like" composition sung or played on an orchestral instrument. The accompaniment should be played on the piano (or guitar) "in the left hand." Particular attention should be directed toward the organization of time. Indications should be made for the desired dynamics and tempo. All compositions should be performed at the same "session." Individual creativity will enhance the learning experience.

VIII. Concepts of the Formal Organization of Music
Principles of Repetition and Contrast

Musical form is the organization of the materials of music. All of the aspects of melody, harmony, tone color, and meter need to be considered to produce a unified whole.

Our Western music seems to be organized for the most part upon the principle of repetition (see again Aaron Copland's comment quoted in Chapter I)—repetition preceded by contrast, repetition by variation, repetition by fugal treatment and repetition by development. These categories of formal organization were first proposed by Aaron Copland in a series of lectures in New York in 1936–1937 and they seem to "make sense" to many musicians.

Fortunately, there are many short, clearly delineated compositions that can illustrate these various categories. Best of all, the principle of repetition evident in these small examples is similar to that employed in large compositions.

52. Twinkle, Twinkle Little Star

Repetition preceded by contrast is evident in Example 52. The A–B–A format here is often presented with the first section repeated (A–A–B–A). This gives still more emphasis to the original material before the appearance of the contrasting section. Melodies such as "Long, Long Ago" and "Old Man River" are written in an A–A–B–A form.

The "theme with variations" is a category of repetition that has been used for centuries. The variations may be varied in melodic, harmonic, metric, textural or timbre content. Twentieth century jazz—from Dixieland to the present day—employs inventive "variations on a theme." Example 53 is a 19th century theme with variations by Carl Maria von Weber for clarinet solo and orchestra. Only the first four measures of the theme and variations are reproduced here.

53. Concertino, op. 26 (Weber)

The simplest example of repetition by fugal treatment is the canon—a composition in which one voice imitates exactly a preceding voice. "Three Blind Mice" and "Row, Row, Row your Boat" are canons or rounds. Example 54 is a German folk song in the form of a canon (or round) for four voices. The figures indicate the entrances of the various voices. For example, Voice 1 begins at the beginning and sings to the end. Voice 2 begins at the beginning when Voice 1 reaches the third measure, etc.

Example 54

Repetition by development is the extension and manipulation of musical ideas as found in the "sonata-allegro" form. The development idea was a product of our classical period and has been expanded and revitalized by many composers of the 19th and 20th centuries. The form itself can perhaps be best explained visually:

Exposition	Development	Recapitulation
A	B	A

The Exposition presents the musical material; the Development allows the composer to manipulate this material utilizing many different musical techniques; the Recapitulation is essentially a repetition of the Exposition.

Example 55

Example 55 illustrates some of the musical manipulations that might be found in a development of the sonata-allegro form.

Example 52 is the folk song, "Twinkle, Twinkle Little Star" in the key of C Major. Example 55 "develops" the theme. Measure 1 is a "fragment" of the first phrase of the song in the key of G. Major (a "transposition" from the original key); measure 2 presents the fragment at a different pitch level (a "sequence"); measure 3 gives us the fragment "upside down" (an "inversion"); measure 4 is a "diminution" of the fragment (shorter note values); the second half of measure 4 and measure 5 are "augmentations" (longer note values); measure 6 is the fragment presented "backwards" ("retrograde"); and measure 7 "modulutes" back to the original key of C Major.

These same modifications of musical material can be utilized in various forms which use repetition by fugal treatment. In other words, the imitation in these compositions is not always exact and is "interrupted" by musical ideas that are transposed, inverted, augmented, etc.

Obviously, there exists Western music not based upon repetition or the traditional forms just discussed. A vocal composition in which the composer has attempted to follow the text in a meaningful way may contain no musical repetition—the song is said to be "through-composed." An instrumental composition which contains extra-musical connotations (programmatic music) may be difficult to analyze in traditional ways. In fact, the composition may well create a form of its own.

Architects and designers attempt to make "form follow function." The composer attempts to make "form follow content." The materials of music cannot be poured into a jug—they must develop in their own way a form which best suits their message.

It may seem odd that the important exercises accompanying this discussion of form in music include the composition of a single phrase and chordal analysis. Perhaps another literary analogy will help explain this combination of discussion-exercise.

A student learning how to write meaningful paragraphs, sentences or even phrases can certainly be aided by reading and analyzing Shakespeare, Milton and Wordsworth. Similarly a student learning to compose music can profit by familiarity through analysis of Bach, Mozart, and Beethoven.

Exercises

1. Key signatures:

   B♭ Major____________
   G♭ Major____________
   B Major____________
   C♯ Major____________
   E♭ Major____________
   d minor ____________
   e minor ____________
   C minor____________
   F minor____________
   B minor____________

2. Give the relative minor to:

   F Major____________
   G Major____________
   A Major____________
   D♭ Major____________
   C♭ Major____________

3. Give the relative major to:

   c minor____________
   e♭ minor____________
   f minor____________
   b minor____________
   g minor____________

4. Build a major scale on:

   E______________________________
   D♭______________________________

5. Build a pure minor scale on:

   E______________________________
   C______________________________

6. Build a harmonic minor scale on:

   C♯______________________________
   G______________________________

7. Build a melodic minor scale (ascending form) on:

   D______________________________
   G♯______________________________

8. Scales

   B♭ is the sixth degree of the ______ major scale
   third degree of the ______ minor scale
   fifth degree of the ______ major scale
   seventh degree of the ______ harmonic minor scale
   fifth degree of the ______ minor scale

9. Triads

   G is the third of the ______ minor triad
   fifth of the ______ diminished triad
   third of the ______ augmented triad
   fifth of the ______ major triad
   third of the ______ major triad

10. Triads in a key

    IV in A♭ Major________
    V in e harmonic minor________
    VII in c harmonic minor______
    III in D Major________
    II in C♯ Major________

11. The II in A Major (spelled ________) normally progresses to ________ (spelled ________) or ________ (spelled ________).

12. The VI in e minor (spelled ________) normally progresses to ________ (spelled ________) or ________ (spelled ________).

13. The VII in A♭ Major (spelled ________) normally progresses to ________ (spelled ________).

14. The IV in d minor (spelled ________) normally progresses to ________ (spelled ________) or ________ (spelled ________).

15. The V in E♭ Major (spelled ________) in a deceptive cadence normally progresses to ________ (spelled ________).

16. The last chord in a half cadence in g minor is ________ (spelled ________).

17. The III in b minor (spelled ________) normally progresses to ________ spelled ________).

18. The dominant chord in c minor is ________ (spelled ________).

19. The subdominant chord in f♯ minor is ________ (spelled ________).

20. The leading tone triad in f minor is ________ (spelled ________).

21. In the following examples, indicate: key; chord choice (roman numeral) classification; type of cadence.

Chorale: Nun ruhen alle Wälder (Bach)

Nocturne, op. 37, no. 1 (Chopin)

Wiegenlied, op. 49, no. 4 (Brahms)

will, wurst du wie- der ge -weckt, Mor- gen
früh, wenn Gott will, wirst du wie - der ge- weckt.

Chorale: Mein Augen schliess ich jetzt in Gottes Namen zu (Bach)

An den Sonnenschein, op. 36, no. 4 (Schumann)

22. Continue using folk song collections to experience tonal and time organization. Emphasize compound time examples. Beat time with your foot or a pencil and use the piano as a "pitch-checking" tool.

Listening Assignment

D. Scarlatti. *Sonatas* (Longo edition) nos. 104, 338, 413
(examples of two-part form)

Mozart. *Eine Kleine Nachtmusik* (third movement)
(example of A–B–A Form)

Bach. *Passacaglia in c minor*
(example of repetition by variation)

Weber. *Concertino for Clarinet and Orchestra op. 26*
(example of theme and variations)

Franck. *Sonata for Violin and Piano in A Major*
(example of repetition by fugal treatment)

Mozart. *Symphony no. 39 in E♭ Major, K. 543* (first movement)
(example of repetition by development)

Composition

d harmonic minor; $\frac{4}{4}$ time; 4 measures

I | 2nd Cl. | 1st Cl. | I ||

The emphasis should continue to be placed upon writing an interesting, pleasing melody above the indicated harmonic structure. The use of the harmonic form of the minor scale will help develop the feeling of "urge" we have for the first class chords to resolve to tonic.

A conscious choice should be made between the second class chords (II, IV) and first class chords (V, VII) in developing the composition.

Tempo and dynamics (and nuances of both of these musical factors) should be indicated.

IX. Seventh Chords
Types and Functions

It is fair to say that the basic harmonic unit of Western music (since at least 1600) is the triad (see Chapter V). And, by simply extending our triads by another third, we create additional harmonic vocabulary called seventh chords. The seventh chords along with the triads are the great bulk of our harmonic material in the music of the 17th, 18th, and 19th centuries. Even much music of the 20th century depends upon these chords for its harmonic structure.

As is true of triads, seventh chords can be built on each step of major and minor scales.

Example 56

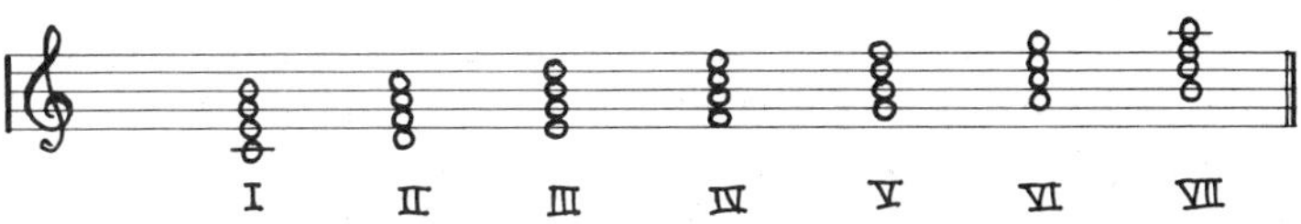

The seventh chords built on pitches of any major scale (Example 56) produce variously constructed chords. For example the seventh chords built on I and IV are made of a major triad and the interval of a major seventh from the root to the seventh of the chord. By definition, these are major seventh chords and are symbolized either by "M^7" or "MM^7" to indicate the major triad and the interval of the major seventh.

The seventh chords formed on II, III and VI of any major scale contain a minor triad and the interval of a minor seventh between root and seventh of the chord. By definition, these are minor seventh chords and are symbolized either by "m^7" or "mm^7" to indicate the minor triad and the interval of the minor seventh.

The most frequently used seventh chord is built on V of any major scale and contains a major triad and the interval of the minor seventh between root and the seventh of the chord. By definition, this is a major–minor seventh chord and is symbolized by "Mm^7" to indicate the major triad and the interval of the minor seventh. Perhaps because of its popularity and because this particular sound can only be formed on V of major keys (assuming we use only those pitches that make up the scale) this seventh chord is also known as the "dominant seventh" chord.

The seventh chord formed on VII of any major scale contains a diminished triad and the interval of the minor seventh between the root and seventh of the chord. By definition, this is a "diminished minor seventh" or a "half-diminished seventh" and is symbolized either by "dm^7" or "½d^7" to indicate the diminished triad and the interval of the minor seventh.

Note that all of these seventh chords have been formed by using only those seven pitches that are found in that particular major scale. They are all by definition, diatonic seventh chords.

Example 57

The diatonic seventh chords that can be formed if we utilize the natural, harmonic and melodic forms of the minor scale can be quite numerous. Among the seventh chords that can be constructed using minor scales that do not appear in the major scale structure are (see Example 57): a I^7 containing a minor triad and a M^7 (I^2 in Example 57); a III^7 containing an augmented triad and a M^7 (III^2 in Example 57); and a VII^7 containing a diminished triad and the interval of a diminished seventh between root and seventh—a "diminished seventh chord" symbolized by "dd^7" or "d^7" to indicate the usage of a diminished triad and the interval of a diminished seventh (VII^2 in Example 57).

From the many diatonic seventh chords that can be formed from our major and minor scales, there are only five types that are frequently used: the M^7 (a major triad and a M^7); the Mm^7 (a major triad and a m^7); the m^7 (a minor triad and a m^7); the ½d^7 (a diminished triad and a m^7); and the d^7 (a diminished triad and a d^7). Example 58 illustrates these frequently used chords built upon the same root.

Example 58

It seems important to note the types of seventh chords formed on V and VII (the first class chords) in major and harmonic minor scales. Since the addition of another third in the "ladder of thirds" that form these chords seems to enhance the "pull" we feel toward the tonal center (the tonic), their frequency of use is pronounced.

Example 59

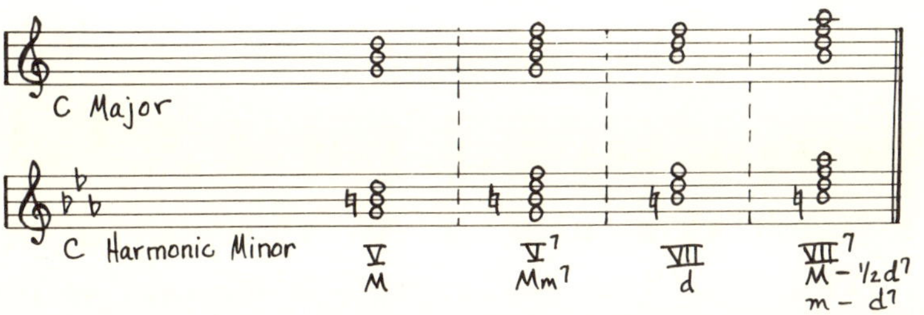

The V and VII triads in both major and harmonic minor keys are the same type (see Example 59). This is also true of the V^7 in both keys. The VII^7 in major keys is a $½d^7$ while the VII^7 in harmonic minor is a d^7 because of the lowered sixth step of the scale. These three sonorities—the Mm^7, the $½d^7$ and the d^7—can be associated with "first class feeling" and fulfill the same function in our music as the V and VII triads.

In fact the function of *all* the diatonic seventh chords is identical with the triads formed on the same root (i.e., both IV^7 and IV are second class chords; both VI^7 and VI are third class chords, etc.). Furthermore, as is true of the various types of triads, a particular sonority can assume the function of different scale degrees. For example, the m^7 built on D can be used as II^7 in C Major, III^7 in B♭ Major, VI^7 in F Major and IV^7 in a harmonic minor, etc.

Exercises

1. Seventh chords:

Key	*Symbol*	*Spelling*	*Type*
E Major	II^7	________	________
B♭ Major	VI^7	________	________
d minor	V^7	________	________
b minor	IV^7	________	________
c♯ minor	VII^7	________	________
E♭ Major	VII^7	________	________

2. "Spelling":

   Spell a Mm^7 on A: ____________
   Spell a M^7 on E: ____________
   Spell a ½d^7 on G♭: ____________
   Spell a d^7 on B: ____________
   Spell a m^7 on D: ____________

3. The V^7 in A Major is a____________(type) spelled____________.

4. The II^7 in g minor is a____________(type) spelled____________.

5. The VI^7 in e minor is a____________(type) spelled____________.

6. The IV^7 in E♭ Major is a____________(type) spelled____________.

7. The III^7 in B Major is a____________(type) spelled____________.

8. The II^7 in E♭ Major (spelled________) normally progresses to________ (spelled________) or________ (spelled________).

9. The VI^7 in d minor (spelled________) normally progresses to________ (spelled________) or________ (spelled________).

10. The VII^7 in E Major (spelled________) normally progresses to________ (spelled________).

11. The IV^7 in e minor (spelled________) normally progresses to________ (spelled________) or________ (spelled________).

12. The V^7 in A Major (spelled________) in a deceptive cadence normally progresses to________ (spelled________).

13. The last chord in a half cadence in b minor is________ (spelled________).

14. The III^7 in g minor (spelled________) normally progresses to________ (spelled________).

15. The dominant seventh chord in f♯ minor is________ (spelled________).

16. The subdominant seventh chord in c minor is________ (spelled________).

17. The leading tone seventh chord in c♯ minor is________ (spelled________).

18. Write the following chords in the following keys—with key signatures. (All minor keys indicate harmonic minor.)

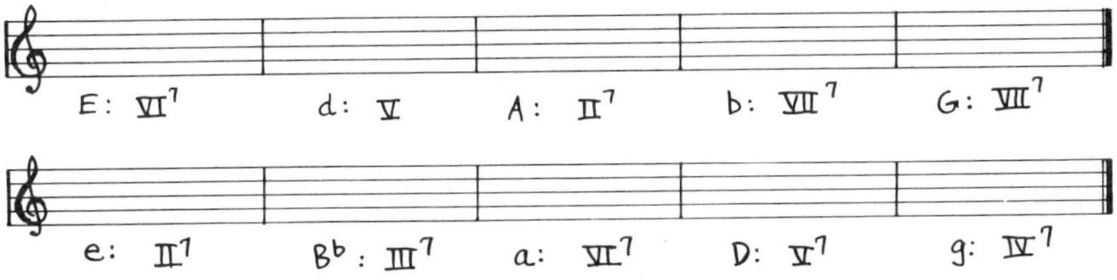

19. Indicate *above* each of the preceding examples the *type* of seventh chord produced.

20. The II^7 in A Major (spelled________) normally progresses to________ (spelled________) or________ (spelled). The II^7 is a________ class chord.

21. The VI^7 in b minor (spelled________) normally progresses to________ (spelled________) or________ (spelled________). The VI^7 is a________ class chord.

22. The VII^7 in A♭ Major (spelled________) normally progresses to________ (spelled________). The VII^7 is a________ class chord.

23. The IV^7 in d minor (spelled________) normally progresses to________ (spelled________) or________ (spelled________). The IV^7 is a________ class chord.

24. The V^7 in E♭ Major (spelled________) in a deceptive cadence normally progresses to________ (spelled________). The V^7 is a________ class chord.

25. The last chord in a half cadence in g minor is________ (spelled______).

26. The III^7 in e minor (spelled________) normally progresses to________ (spelled________). The III^7 is a________ class chord.

27. The dominant seventh chord in c minor is________ (spelled________).

28. The subdominant seventh chord in f♯ minor is________ (spelled ________).

29. The leading tone seventh chord in g♯ minor is________ (spelled ________).

30. Give the key center and make a chordal analysis of the following musical excerpts. Indicate *types* of seventh chords.

Sonata for Piano, K. 533 (Mozart)

Chorale: Werde munter, mein Gemüte (Bach)

Sonatina for Piano, op. 88, no. 3 (Kuhlau)

Sonata for Violin and Piano, K. 379 (Mozart)

Waltz, op. 69, no. 2 (Chopin)

Sonata for Piano, op. 31, no. 2 (Beethoven)

Waltz, op. 18a, no. 5 (Schubert)

31. Continue sight singing and metric practice. Do not neglect compositions in minor keys and compound time.

Listening Assignment

Beethoven. *Sonata for Violin and Piano,* op. 24

Brahms. *Variations on a Theme of Haydn,* op. 56a

Composition

B♭ Major $\frac{9}{8}$ | I | VI^7 | second class, seventh chord (II^7 or IV^7) | first class, seventh chord (V^7 or VII^7) | I ||

The melodic line is still all important. Indicate articulations as well as nuances of tempo and dynamics. Experiment in the choice of first and second class seventh chords. The progressions as finalized *will* make a difference.

X. Nonchord Tones
Types and Functions

Composing musical melodies involves the use of many pitches that are additions to the basic harmonic structure. These "nonchord" tones fulfill three important functions: they beautify, ornament and decorate; they add tension or suspense; they create metric interest.

Nonchord tones can be any pitch from the chromatic scale and need not be limited to just the pitches of any given key. Traditionally, nonchord tones fit the various categories illustrated below. These examples should be played or sung to understand the musical meanings of the nonchord tones.

Passing Tone

60. Chorale: Jesus selbst, mein Licht, mein Leben (Bach)

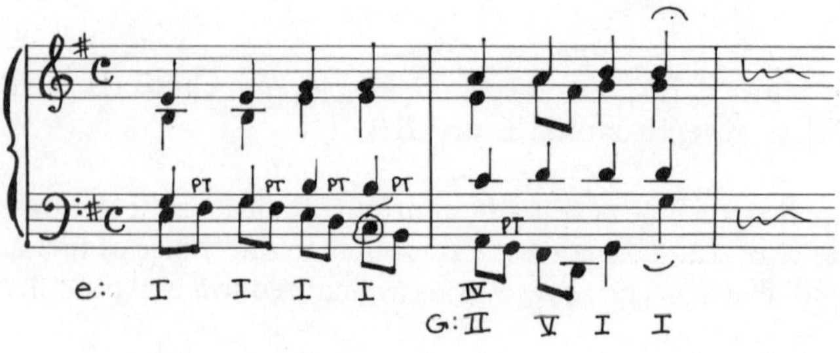

61. Sonata for Piano, op. 10, no. 3 (Beethoven)

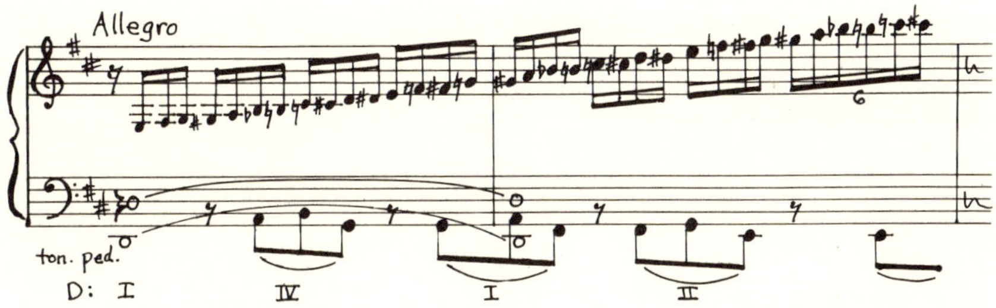

Fortunately, the categories of nonchord tones aptly describe the use of the added pitches. Passing tones "pass" between or connect chord tones. Note the passing tones (PT) in the bass line of Example 60 are both on the beat and (in measure 1, beat 4) off the beat. The passing tones in the top staff of Example 61 use pitches "outside" the key center and there is more than one passing tone between chord tones.

Neighboring Tone

62. Chorale: Alle Menschen müssen sterben (Bach)

63. Carnaval, op. 9, no. 5, Eusebius (Schumann)

The Bach chorale example above contains passing tones and a neighboring tone (NT) in the tenor (in the second measure). As its name implies, a neighboring tone returns to the pitch from which it departed. This departure can be either above or below the chord tone and of course it can be chromatically inflected. (See Example 63.)

Anticipation

64. Concerto Grosso, op. 6, no. 5 (Handel)

65. Chorale: Aufmeinen lieben Gott (Bach)

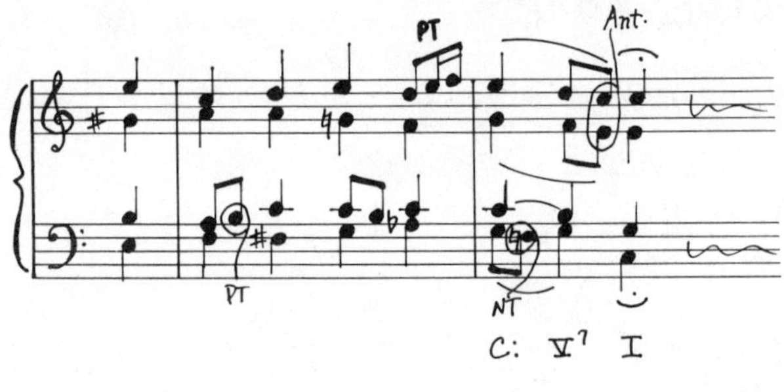

66. Chorale: Alles ist an Gottes Segen (Bach)

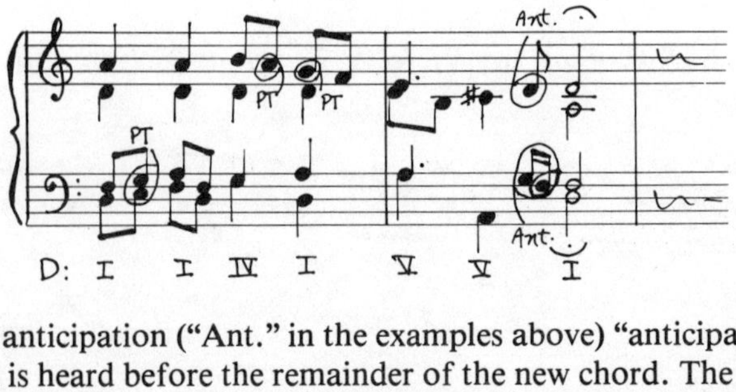

The anticipation ("Ant." in the examples above) "anticipates" a chord change and is heard before the remainder of the new chord. The three examples of anticipations above illustrate their use at cadences, their most frequent function. Anticipations decorate the melodic line and also seem to add tension, which makes the arrival of the cadential chord even more welcome.

Suspension

67. Sonata for Piano, K. 533 (Mozart)

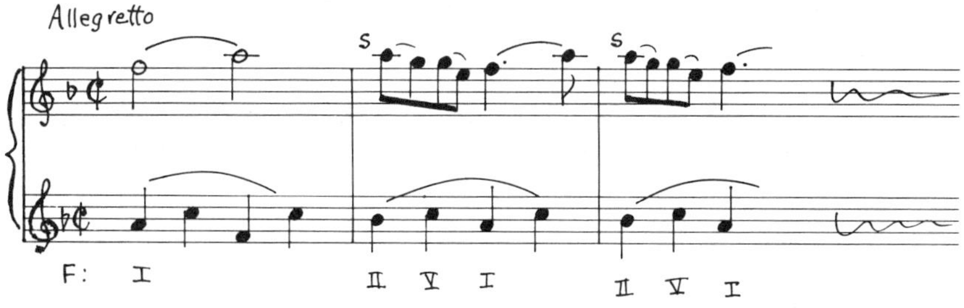

68. Prelude, op. 28, no. 13 (Chopin)

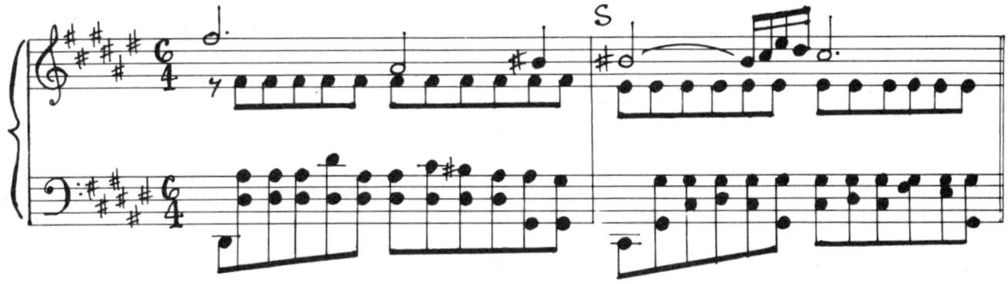

69. Sonata for Piano, op. 27, no. 2 (Beethoven)

70. *Sonata for Piano, no. 7* (Haydn)

The suspension can be considered the opposite of the anticipation in that it *delays* harmonic completion in a progression. As is true of the anticipation, the suspension not only ornaments the melodic line but creates tension. More than ever these musical examples should be played or sung to fully appreciate the effect of these nonchord tones. In the examples above, the "s" indicates the suspension.

Appoggiatura or Leaning Tone

71. *Sonata for Piano, K. 331* (Mozart)

72. *Sonata for Piano, op. 7* (Beethoven)

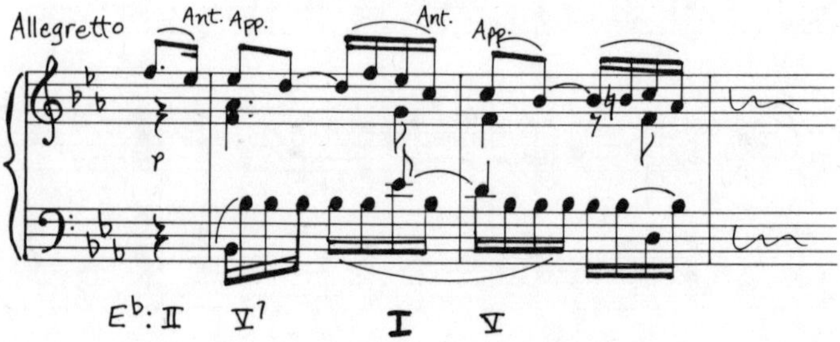

73. Concerto for Piano, no. 2, op. 83 (Brahms)

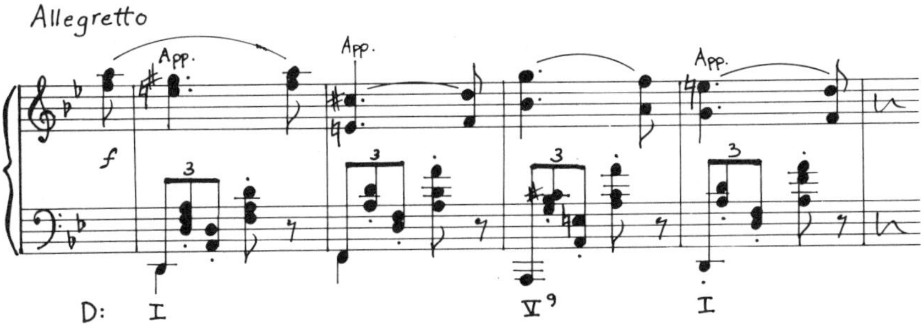

The appoggiatura, or leaning tone, is another "tension-provoking" nonchord tone. As Examples 71, 72, 73 illustrate, the leaning tone frequently occurs on a metrically strong part of the measure and need not be a diatonic pitch.

Pedal Tone

74. Prelude no. 1, Well-Tempered Clavier, Book 1 (Bach)

75. Sonatina for Piano, op. 36, no. 4 (Clementi)

A pedal tone is simply a sustained pitch through a series of chord changes. The pedal may be below, above or in the mid-pitch range of these chords and in many situations it may be more than one pitch. The previous examples illustrate the pedal in the bass. The repeated octave pedal in Example 75 is a typical pianistic technique to sustain the tonic pitch throughout the four measures.

There are other less frequently used categories of nonchord tones but the reasons for their usage are the same as the types of nonchord tones discussed above. These added notes ornament and/or add tension and metric interest to the musical material—a function long appreciated in the development of Western music.

Exercises

Make a chordal analysis of the following musical excerpts. Identify the non-chord tones by category.

1. *Chorale: Ach Gott, erhör mein Seufzen und Wehklagen* (Bach)

2. *Sonatina for Piano in G Major* (Haydn)

3. *Country Dance no. 7, Wo O11* (Beethoven)

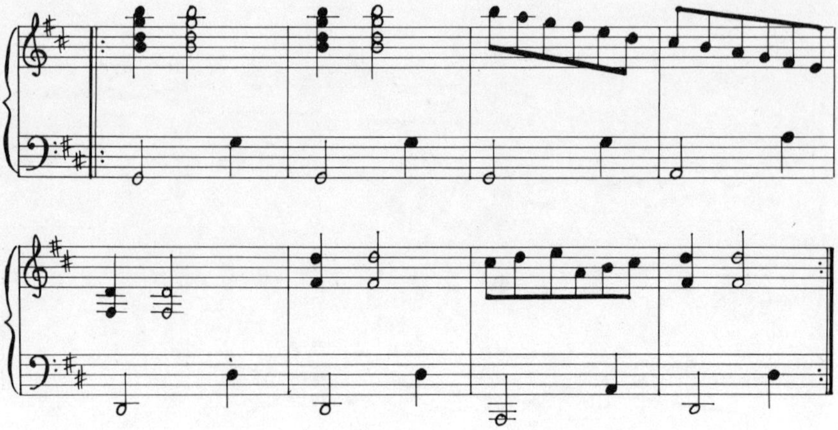

4. *Concerto for Piano and Orchestra, K.467* (Mozart)

*The alto clef *used for the viola indicates that middle C is on the third line. The pitches in the first measure are C, E and G. Contrabasso (stringbass) sounds an octave below the cello.*

5. *Valse (Posthumous)* (Chopin)

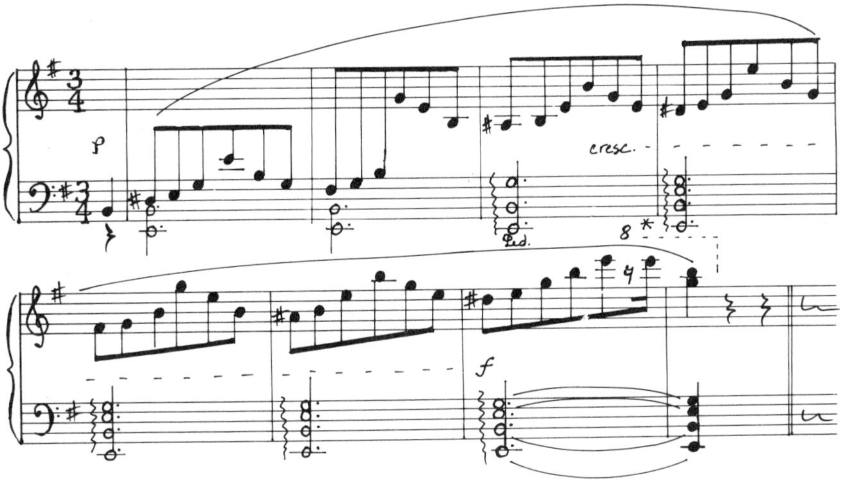

6. As practice in singing folk songs is continued, special attention should be directed to nonchord tones.

Listening Assignment

Mozart. *Concerto for Piano and Orchestra* in C Major, K. 467

Chopin. Etudes, op. 10 and op. 25

Shubert. *Symphony no. 8* in b minor

Composition

a harmonic minor; $\frac{3}{4}$ time

I | VI | II^7 | VII^7 | I | V ||

Emphasize chromatic nonchord tones in the melody to ornament and add tension. The half cadence should stimulate tension-producing ideas.

XI. Common Chord and Phrase Modulation; Change of Mode

Process and Function

The principle of repetition which organizes a great part of our music also carries with it the idea of contrast and/or variety. The pleasure experienced upon the eventual return of a familiar musical thought is enhanced by these excursions from the original material by the composer.

One of the very important musical tools used to create contrast or variety is modulation, or change of key. The technique of modulation is so all-pervasive that it is difficult to find examples of music since 1600 that do *not* modulate. It is safe to say that except for some extremely short compositions all of our music modulates in some way.

Modulation is most frequently effected through the use of a "common chord." A common chord has a function in the original key center and a different function in the new key center—a C major triad may be used as I in the key of C Major and it can also assume the role of IV in the key of G Major. The ability of a single chord to assume different functions in various key centers is the basis for creating common chord modulations.

76. Chorale: Ach bleib bei uns, Herr Jesu Christ (Bach)

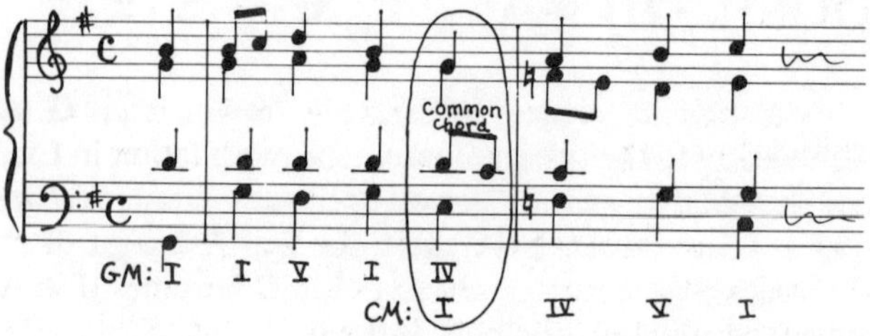

Example 76 illustrates a modulation from G Major to C Major by the use of a common chord—the C major triad, which functions as both IV in G Major and I in C Major.

Example 76 also illustrates clearly the three processes necessary to effect this modulation: establish the original key center, use a common chord, and establish the new key center.

The C major triad is not the only common chord available to connect these two key centers.

Example 77

In Example 77, the triads formed on the scale steps of the G Major scale indicate that four of the possible seven triads can also function in the C Major key center. Any of these double-function chords could be the common chord between these two keys.

78. Sonata for Piano, K. 284 (Mozart)

The modulation illustrated in Example 76 was from G Major to C Major—a modulation to the subdominant. The modulation in Example 78 is from D Major to A Major—a modulation to the dominant, perhaps the most frequent of all in tonal music. Note again the establishment of the original key center (D Major); the common chord (VI in D becomes II in A); and the establishment of the new key center (A Major).

Both examples 76 and 78 contain modulations to "closely related keys" (i.e., key centers that are no more than one sharp or flat removed from the original key). For example, the closely related keys to C Major (no sharps or flats in the key signature) are F Major and d minor (one flat in the key signature), G Major and e minor (one sharp in the key signature), and a minor (the same key signature as C Major). The closely related keys to f♯ minor (three sharps in the key signature) would be D Major and b minor (two sharps in the key signature); E Major and c♯ minor (four sharps in the key signature), and A Major (the same key signature as f♯ minor).

Common chord modulation between any two closely related keys can be easily effected. To modulate from C Major to d minor, II in C can become I in d; to modulate from C Major to e minor, III in C can become I in e, etc. Perhaps the illustration below will be helpful in quickly identifying closely related keys. Simply place the tonic of the original key at the top of the center column and list the other five key centers following the pattern of the "circle of fifths" (see Chapter III).

If D Major is the original key center, the closely related keys are:

one sharp	*two sharps*	*three sharps*
G	D	A
e	b	f♯

If f minor is the original key center, the closely related keys are:

three flats	*four flats*	*five flats*
c	f	b♭
E♭	A♭	G♭

Phrase modulation occurs when the new phrase (or section) simply begins in a different key center. Following the completion of a musical unit (phrase, section, etc.) composers frequently change key. The ear readily accepts this kind of modulatory logic.

79. Chorale: Was fürchst du, Feind Herodes, sehr (Bach)

80. *Chorale: Ach wie flüchtig, ach wie nichtig* (Bach)

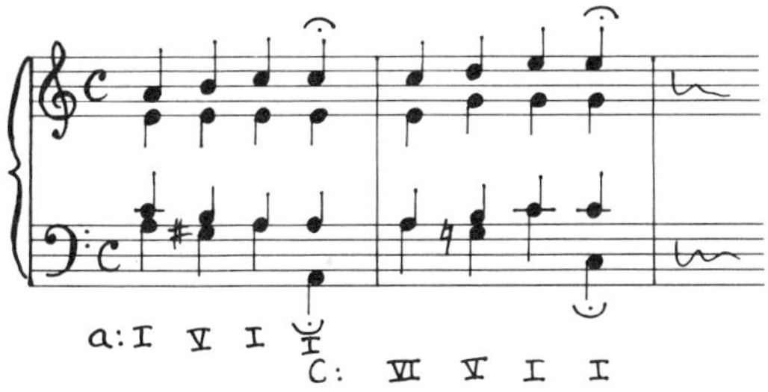

In the two examples above taken from the beginnings of chorales, potential common chords can be identified—the first chord of the second phrase of Example 79 could be f I or C IV and the first chord of the second phrase of Example 80 could be a I or C VI. As a matter of practical musicianship, however, both examples would probably be considered phrase modulations since the new key is established at the beginnings of the phrases. The C Major chord concluding Example 79 illustrates a common practice of the 18th century to end a phrase or section in major although the composition is in minor. The final major triad is called the "Picardy Third."

81. *Rondo for Piano, K. 485* (Mozart)

Example 81 illustrates a phrase modulation (from e minor to C Major) between sections of a much longer composition—a fairly common practice from the 18th century to the present day.

Although a change of mode (from major to minor or visa versa) does not provide the same quality of variety that changing the key center can, this important change of "color" is widely used both within phrases or sections and between them.

The "Minuetto" of Mozart's famous symphony in g minor (no. 40, K. 550) is a typical example of a change of mode between sections. The original key of the movement is g minor; the Trio is in G Major and, of course, the return to the beginning section is in g minor.

82. *Sonata for Piano, K. 279* (Mozart)

83. *Sonata for Piano, op. 53* (Beethoven)

84. *Dichterliebe, op. 48* (Schumann)

85. Intermezzo for Piano, op. 119, no. 3 (Brahms)

The change of mode within the phrase or section (see examples 82, 83, 84 and 85) involves the interchange of the third and sixth scale degrees between the major and minor scales constructed upon the same pitch.

Example 86 compares the C Major and harmonic minor scales. Note that the scales differ on the third and sixth degrees. These notes are (understandably) called the "modal" degrees because they delineate the differences between the major and minor modes.

Example 86

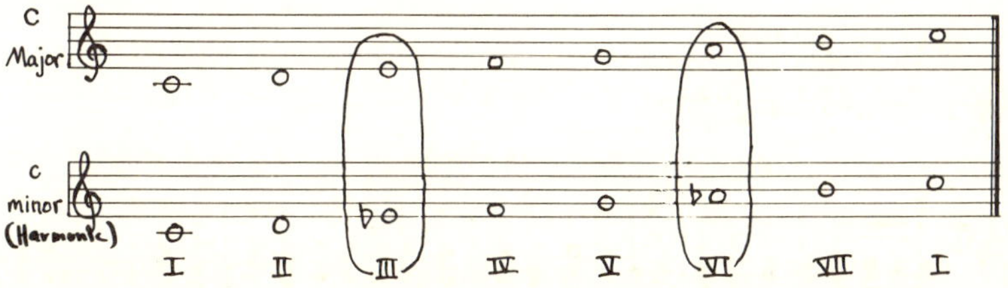

Change of mode contributes to an expansion of the key system accessible for modulation. For example, changing mode from C Major to c minor brings five new closely related keys to the original C Major key center. The diagram on the next page illustrates this expansion.

e	a	d
G	C	F
	↕	
g	c	f
B♭	E♭	A♭

The inclusion of the parallel mode concept leads to variety in color and mood as well as to expansion of modulatory goals.

There are other well established techniques for accomplishing effective modulations through the use of secondary dominants and other altered chords. These procedures will be examined as each of the new chord types are presented.

Exercises

1. List all common chords for the following modulations:

a minor	to	F Major
A♭ Major	to	c minor
G Major	to	D Major
B♭ Major	to	g minor
c♯ minor	to	f♯ minor

2. List the modal scale degrees in the following keys:

   A♭ Major
   e minor
   D Major
   g minor

3. List the roman numeral functions of the following diatonic triads in all possible key centers.

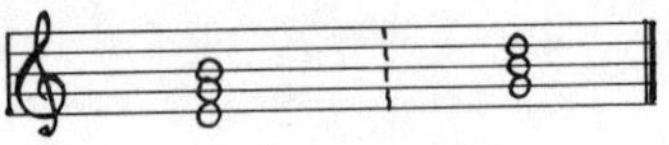

4. List the common chord functions of the following triads in as many modulations as possible.

5. Diagram with roman numerals and chord spellings the following common chord modulations. Each modulation should establish the original key, use a common chord, and establish the new key.

D Major to its subdominant ______________________________

F Major to its dominant ______________________________

g minor to its relative major ______________________________

E♭ Major to its relative minor ______________________________

A Major to its parallel minor (i.e., the minor key whose tonic is also "A")______________________________

6. Give the original key center, make chordal analysis and indicate modulations in the following musical excerpts.

Sonatina for Piano, op. 36, no. 4 (Clementi)

Album for the Young, op. 68 (Schumann)

Heidenrosein op. 3, no. 3 (Schubert)

Lieblich
Sah ein Knab' ein Rös-lein steh'n, Rös-lein auf der Hei - den.
War so jung und mor-gen schön, lief er schnell, es nah' zu seh'n,

Dido and Aeneas (Purcell)

7. Sightsinging practice should now include folk songs that modulate. It is now especially important to check pitches with the piano.

Listening Assignment

Beethoven. *Sonata for Piano in C Major, op. 53*

Brahms. *Intermezzo in C Major, op. 119, no. 3*

Mozart. *Symphony no. 40 in g minor, K. 550*

Composition

B♭ Major; $\frac{4}{2}$ time; 4 measures

I | 2nd Cl. | 1st Cl. | I | VI |
F; II | 1st Cl. | I ||

Make conscious choices (i.e., experiment) between the various second and first class chords. The time signature of $\frac{4}{2}$ is simply an inflation of note values and will sound exactly like $\frac{4}{4}$ time.

G Major; $\frac{6}{8}$ time

I | VI | IV | II^7 | V | VII^7 | I | I || Fine

C Major: I | IV^7 | VII | I |
G M: IV | V^7 | I | IV^7 | V || D.C.

The composition above can be completed in two assignments. The complete composition is in A–B–A form. The first section is also the last section ("D.C." indicates a return to the beginning with the final cadence at "Fine"). The second section begins with a phrase modulation to C Major and includes a common chord modulation back to G Major. The second section should be in contrast to the first section in as many ways as your good taste in music will allow. For example, the melodic line could be decidedly different from your first tune; the accompaniment could be in a different style; the tempo dynamics and meter could change, and so on.

XII. Secondary Dominants
Structures and Functions

The evident affinity of composers for the dominant–tonic (or first class to tonic) relationship is obvious in the music of the 17th, 18th and 19th centuries—and beyond. It is also possible to construct this same relationship on any step of the scale so that many triads within a key center can "masquerade" as a tonic chord (approached by its own first class chord) on a temporary basis.

87. Symphony no. 1, op. 21 (Beethoven)

Although the use of secondary dominants in Example 87 adds "extra" pitches (that is, added accidentals) the feeling for the original key center is enhanced by giving more importance to each *temporary tonic* as it progresses towards the *original tonic* in measure 6.

These additional first class–tonic relationships seem never to detract

88. Eine kleine Nachtmusik, K. 525 (Mozart)

89. Chorale: Cantata no. 140, Wachet auf, Ruft uns die Stimme (Bach)

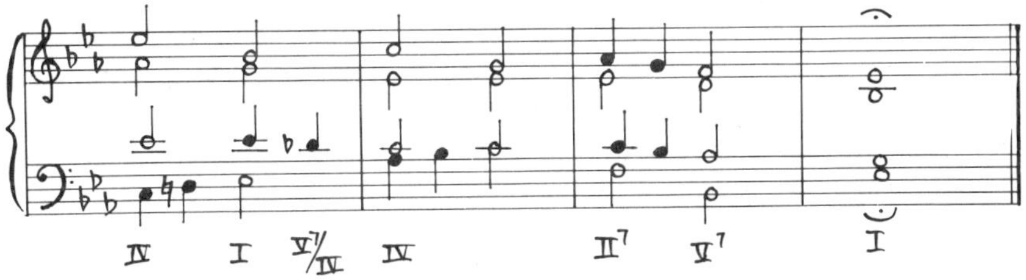

90. Symphony no. 5, D 485 (Schubert)

from the original tonic feeling but rather add a further dimension and support to the key center. Note examples 88, 89, and 90.

Secondary dominants are constructed and function in all the ways that "original" dominants function. A secondary dominant built a perfect fifth above its temporary tonic can be either a major triad or a major minor seventh chord. The temporary tonic can be any major or minor triad.

Example 91

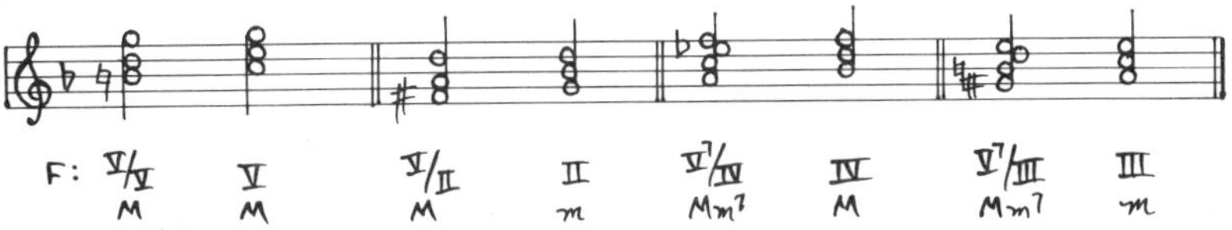

Example 91 illustrates the functions of secondary dominants that are either V or V^7 in their relationship to a temporary tonic. The V/V is a major triad built a perfect fifth above its temporary major tonic—V in F Major. It follows that the V/II will also be a major triad built a perfect fifth above its temporary tonic even though the II is a minor tonic. In other words V chords of either a major or harmonic minor key center are identical—they are major triads built a perfect fifth above the tonic.

The V^7/IV and the V^7/III are also identically formed—major minor seventh chords built a perfect fifth above their temporary tonics. This, of course, is true of V^7 chords in any major or harmonic minor key.

Example 92

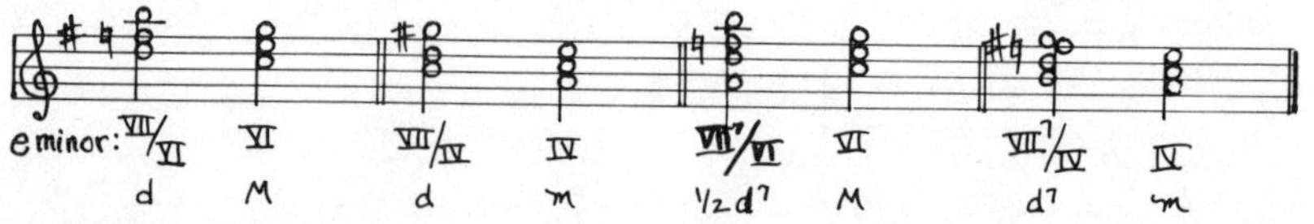

VII and VII^7 chords are also first class chords. In this capacity they are used as secondary dominants.

Example 92 illustrates the functions of secondary dominants that are either VII or VII^7 in their relationship to a temporary tonic. The VII/VI is a diminished triad built a minor second below its temporary major tonic. The VII/IV is identically constructed although it resolves to a temporary minor tonic. Again, this follows the structure and function of VII chords in both major and harmonic minor key centers.

Although the VII^7 in a major key center is a ½d^7 and the VII^7 in a harmonic minor key center is a d^7, the practice of composers has been to use the d^7, whose root is a minor second below its temporary tonic much more frequently—whether or not the chord of resolution is a major or minor triad.

In all the above examples the chords of resolution have been either major or minor triads which conform to the structure of tonic chords in major and harmonic minor key centers. Gradually, however, as the harmonic vocabulary increased during the 19th century, the chord of resolution was not always a substitute for a tonic chord and there are many examples of secondary dominants leading to chords other than the traditional major or minor triads.

Another dimension in the use of secondary dominants is their function in producing a permanent modulation rather than resolving to a temporary tonic. Once the dominant-tonic relationship has been established the lasting modulation can be effected by simply staying in the new key center of the "temporary tonic" or in utilizing another function of the same chord.

93. *Chorale: Nun preiset alle Gottes Barmheizigkeit* (Bach)

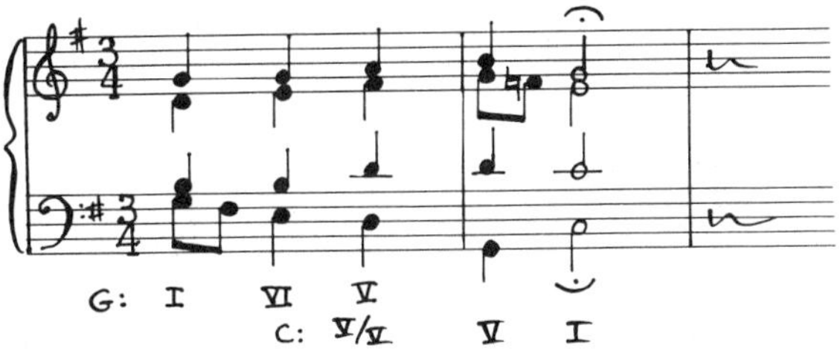

94. *Chorale: Du grosser Schmerzensmann* (Bach)

95. *Sonata for Piano, op. 13* (Beethoven)

96. Mazurka, op. 59, no. 2 (Chopin)

Chordal analysis of the preceding examples illustrate various modulatory uses of secondary dominants. Although this usage almost always produces a chromatic progression, the effectiveness of the modulation still depends upon the positive establishment of the new key center.

Exercises

1. Sing major triads, Mm^7, $\frac{1}{2}d^7$ and d^7 chords on the same root.
2. Sing major triads, Mm^7, $\frac{1}{2}d^7$ and d^7 chords resolving to major or minor triads.
3. Secondary dominants:

		Chord of Resolution (temporary tonic)
V^7/IV in G+	________	________
V/II in B♭ +	________	________
V^7/V in D+	________	________
V/VI in A+	________	________
V^7/III in E♭ +	________	________

V/V in d – ________ ________
V^7/IV in e – ________ ________
V/VI in c – ________ ________
V^7/III in b – ________ ________
V/V in a – ________ ________

4. V/V in b – ________
c♯ – ________
E + ________
A♭ + ________
F♯ + ________

5. V/II in G + ________
F + ________
D + ________
B + ________
G♭ + ________

6. V^7/VI in A + ________
D + ________
B♭ + ________
e – ________
a – ________

7. V^7/III in G + ________
D + ________
c♯ – ________
f♯ – ________
B♭ + ________

8. V^7/IV in e – ________
c – ________
g – ________
E♭ + ________
A + ________

9. V^7/V in f – ________
d – ________
g – ________
e – ________
b – ________

10. Secondary dominants:

11. VII/V in f– ________
d– ________
g– ________
e– ________
b– ________

12. VII/II in e– ________
c– ________
g– ________
E♭ + ________
A + ________

13. VII^7/VI in A + ________
D + ________
B♭ + ________
e– ________
a– ________

14. VII/III in G + ________
D + ________
c♯ – ________
f♯ – ________
B♭ + ________

15. VII^7/IV in b– ________
c♯ – ________
E + ________
A♭ + ________
F♯ + ________

16. VII^7/V in G + ________
F + ________
D + ________
B + ________
G♭ + ________

17. Give the original key center and make chordal analysis in the following musical excerpts.

String Quartet, op. 76, no. 5 (Haydn)

Sonata for Piano, op. 7 (Beethoven)

Variations sur un Theme rococo, op. 33 (Tchaikovsky)

Listing Assignment

Beethoven, *Piano Concerto no. 5 in E Flat Major, op. 73*

Chopin. *Mazurka in A Flat Major, op. 24, no. 3*

Schubert. *Symphony no. 5, in B Flat Major*

Composition

F Major; $\frac{3}{4}$ time; 8 measures

I | III | VI | V^7/IV | VII^7/V | V | I ||

g minor; $\frac{9}{8}$ time; 8 measures

I | VI | VII/IV | IV |
c: I | II^7 | V/V | V^7 | I ||

Strive constantly for interesting and "memorable" melodic material. In many ways, the harmonic structures should be a means to this end.

XIII. The Neapolitan Chord
Structure and Functions

Another frequently used altered chord is the major triad built on the lowered second step of major or minor scales. The so-called "Neapolitan" chord was much used by the operatic composers of 17th century Naples (hence its name) and seems to have been used originally in minor keys.

Example 97

As Example 97 illustrates, a major triad formed on the lowered second step of a minor scale needs only one accidental. The major triad formed on the lowered second step of a major scale requires two accidentals—the lowered second step and the lowered sixth step to form the major triad.

In either scale, the Neapolitan chord (symbolized "N") is usually a second class chord and frequently progresses to first class. Example 98 is useful in cataloguing the various types of sounds now available in second class chords.

Example 98

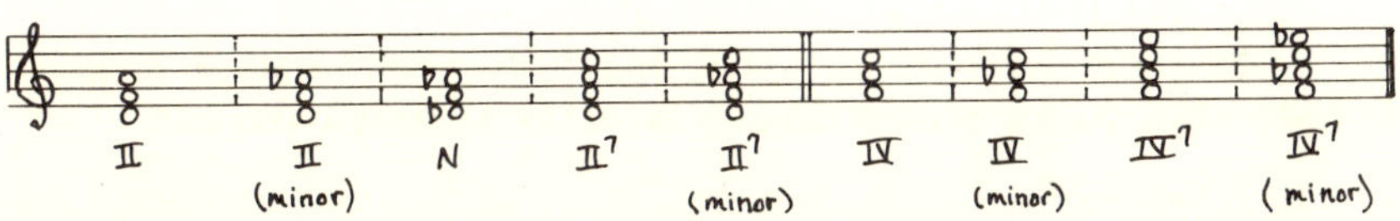

If the second class chords from the parallel minor are "borrowed" (see Chapter X), a large spectrum of various triads and seventh chords is available to "color" melodic material. In a very real sense, the combination of borrowed and altered chords when added to any given key center tends to expand seven note major or minor scales to the 12 notes available in the complete chromatic scale.

The following examples illustrate some of the various ways the Neapolitan chord has been used by some important composers.

99. Quintet for Strings, K. 516 (Mozart)

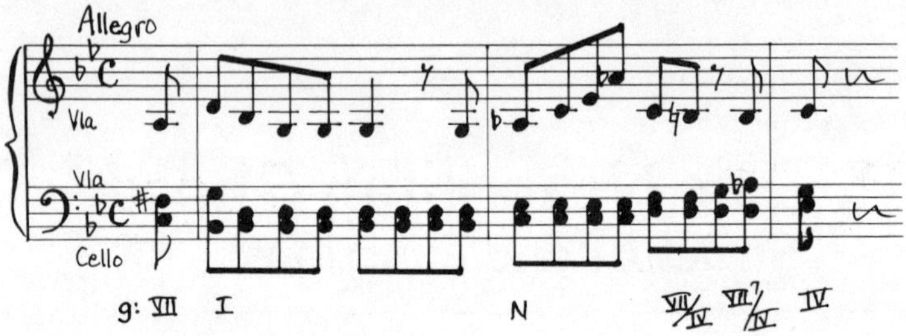

100. Sonata for Piano, op. 27, no. 2 (Beethoven)

101. Mazurka, op. 7, no. 2 (Chopin)

102. Waltz for Piano, op. 124, no. 4 (Schumann)

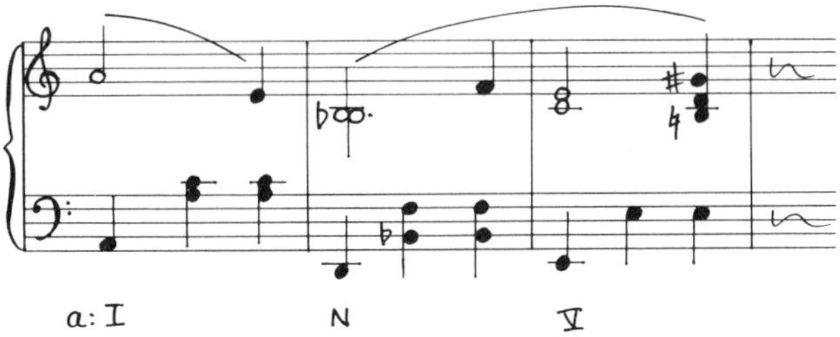

Note that the Neapolitan chord may be preceded by its own secondary dominant (Example 101) and may proceed to other altered chords or first or second class chords.

As is true of the secondary dominants, Neapolitan chords may be used to modulate. Since N is a major triad, it can assume the function of any diatonic major triad in either major or minor tonalities. And, of course, any diatonic major triad can assume the function of a Neapolitan chord in a different tonality. For example, VI in f minor (D♭ FA♭) can become N in C Major. Or N in c minor (D♭ FA♭) can become IV in A♭ Major.

103. Erlkönig, op. 1 (Schubert)

104. Prelude, op. 28, no. 6 (Chopin)

105. Sonata for Piano, op. 14, no. 1 (Beethoven)

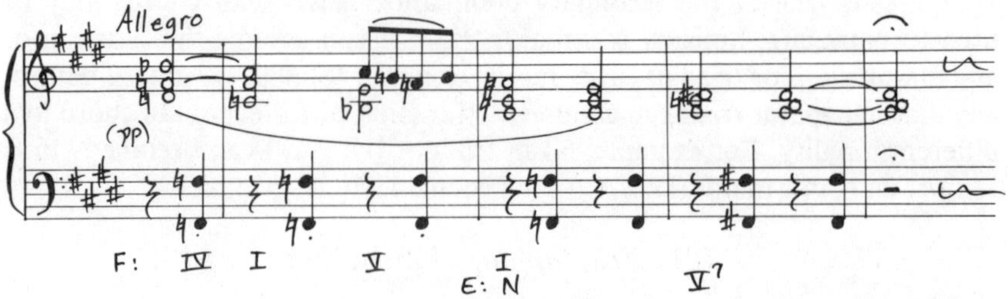

The above examples illustrate the modulatory function of the Neapolitan chord as used by Chopin, Schubert and Beethoven. Note that the process of common chord modulation is the same when either an altered chord or a diatonic chord is used (see Chapter XI).

Exercises

1. Diagram with roman numerals and chord spellings the following common chord modulations. Each modulation should use either a secondary dominant or the Neapolitan chord as the common chord.

G Major	to	F♯ Major
B♭ Major	to	D Major
e minor	to	c minor
c minor	to	F Major

2. Give key centers and make chordal analysis in the following musical excerpts:

Chorale: Ach Gott, vom Himmel sieh' darein (Bach)

Variations for Piano on "God Save the King" (Beethoven)

Sonata for Piano, op. 53 (Beethoven)

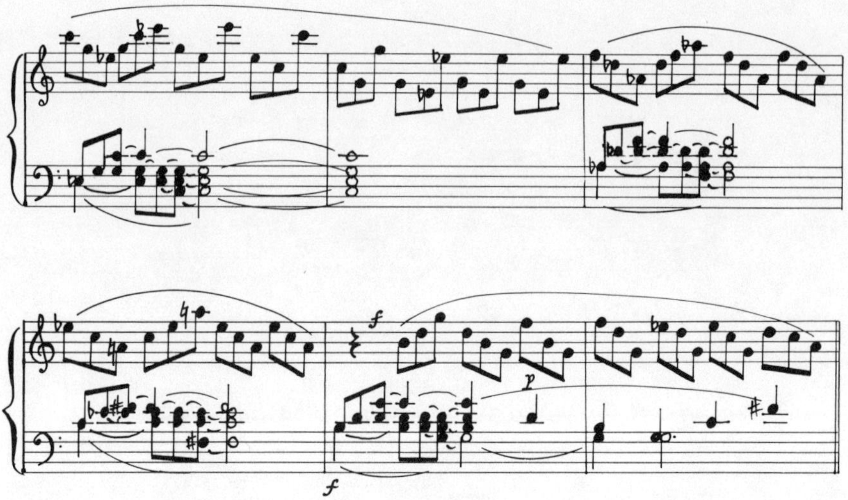

Sonatina for Violin and Piano, op. 137, no. 2 (Schubert)

Nocturne, op. 55, no. 1 (Chopin)

3. Spell Neapolitan chords in the following keys:

D Major ________________
e minor ________________
f♯ minor ________________
B♭ Major ________________
c minor ________________
G Major ________________
A Major ________________
E♭ Major ________________
d minor ________________
b minor ________________

4. Sightsinging practice should include singing all four parts of the preceding Bach example and the uppermost parts of the other preceding examples by Beethoven, Schubert and Chopin.

Listening Assignment

Schumann. *Symphony no. 1* in B Flat Major, op. 38

Brahms. *Academic Festival Overture,* op. 80

Composition

c minor; $\frac{6}{8}$ time

I | VI^7 | N | V | I | VII^7/IV | IV
f: I | V^7 | I ||

A Major; $\frac{4}{4}$ time

I | VII^7/VI VI | N
F: IV | N | V^7 | I ||

It is important to sing the melodies you have created. Are they singable? Do they seem to make balanced phrases?

XIV. The Augmented Sixth Chords
Italian, German and French

Altered chords of still another category contain the interval of the augmented sixth. As is true of the Neapolitan chord, the chords of the augmented sixth usually progress to first class chords and can be used to modulate. For no apparent reason, the three augmented sixth chords are known respectively as Italian, German and French. Example 106 illustrates these chords in the key of C Major.

Example 106

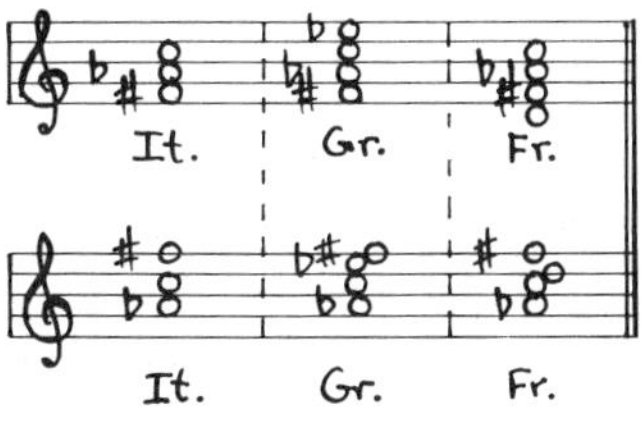

Because these chords were originally used in inverted form (see second line of the above example), the interval of the augmented sixth—from A♭ up to F♯—was prominent. Today's usage could also be in root position which would produce the interval of the diminished third—F♯ up to A♭.

In any major key center, the Italian augmented sixth chord can be thought of as a IV with a ♯4 and a ♭6. In any minor key center, only one altered note is necessary to produce the same sonority—IV with a ♯4.

In any major key center, the German augmented sixth chord can be thought of as a IV^7 with a ♯4, ♭6 and ♭3. In any minor key center, only one altered note is necessary to produce the same sonority—IV^7 with a ♯4.

In any major key center, the French augmented sixth chord can be thought of as a II^7 with a ♯4 and ♭6. In any minor key center only one altered note is necessary to produce the same sonority—II^7 with a ♯4. Example 107 shows the alteration necessary to produce these three chords in both C Major and c minor.

Example 107

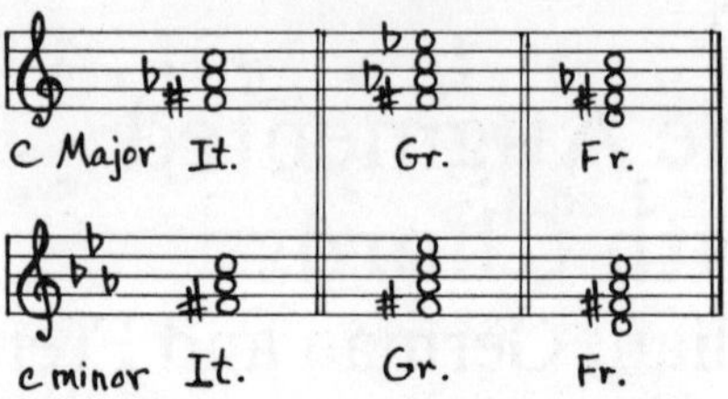

In either major or minor key centers, the interval of the augmented sixth (or diminished third) tends to resolve to the dominant of the key. That is, the augmented sixth moves to the octave and the diminished third to the unison—see Example 108. The ♯4 seems to act as a leading tone to the dominant.

Example 108

With the addition of the chords of the augmented sixth to the previous inventory of chords leading to the dominant (i.e., second class chords) the "harmonic color" possibilities are many and varied. Example 109 illustrates these chords in C Major. Obviously, all these possibilities exist in all major and minor key centers.

Example 109

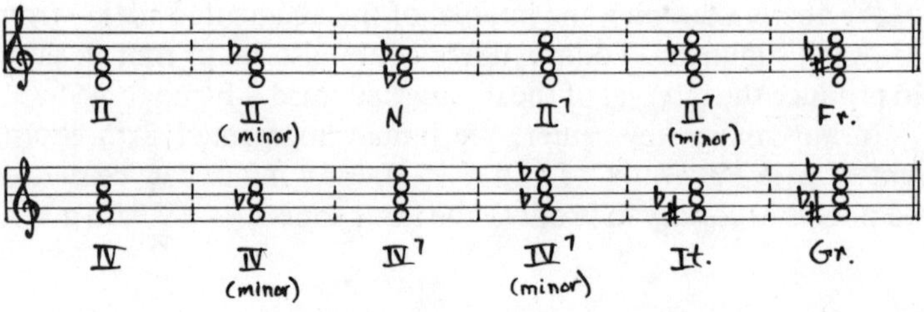

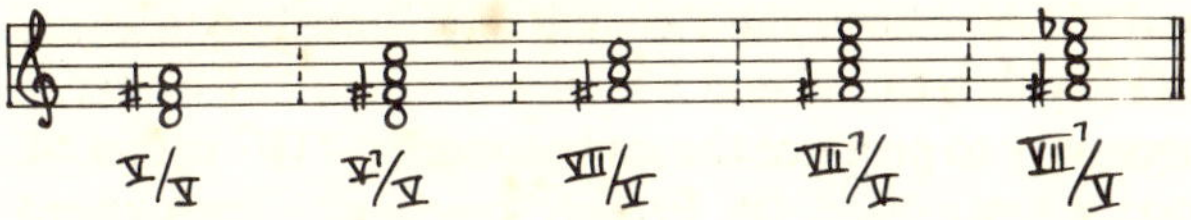

The following examples serve to elucidate the use of the various augmented sixth chords in different musical settings and times.

110. Chorale: Ich hab' mein' Sach' Gott heimgestellt (Bach)

111. Fantasia for Piano, K. 475 (Mozart)

112. Symphony no. 5, op. 67 (Beethoven)

113. Nocturne, op. 48, no. 2 (Chopin)

114. Mazurka, op. 7, no. 2 (Chopin)

115. Tristan und Isolde: Prelude (Wagner)

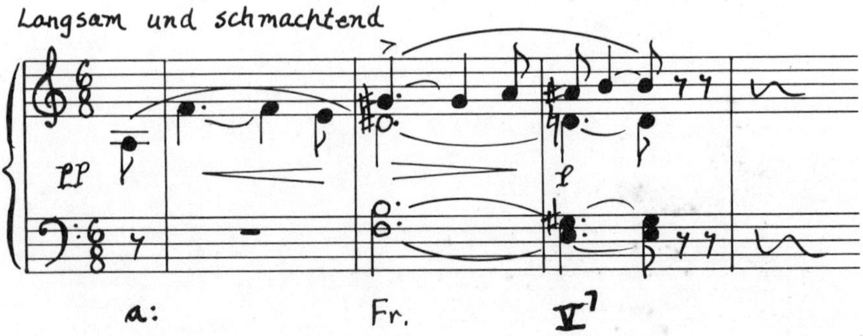

Because the German and Italian augmented sixth chords sound like a Mm^7 chord – and can be respelled as one enharmonically (see Example 116) – they can be used as a common chord and become a V^7 or any secondary dominant seventh chord. And, of course, any Mm^7 chord can be respelled as either a German or Italian augmented sixth chord.

Example 116

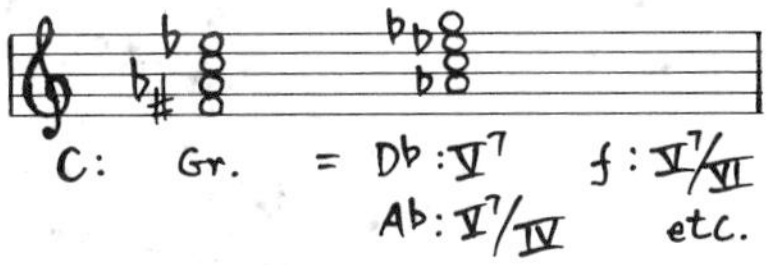

Example 117 contains a common chord in measure 4 which is V⁷/IV in E♭ Major (E♭–G–B♭–D♭) which becomes the German augmented sixth chord in G Major (C♯–E♭–G–B♭). Obviously, this technique makes possible common chord modulation to key centers that are "related" only in terms of their various altered chords. They may have no diatonic similarity (see Example 116; C Major and D♭ Major).

117. String Quartet, op. 76, no. 3 (Haydn)

Exercises

Locate and label all the altered chords (secondary dominants, Neapolitan chord, augmented sixth chords) in the following musical excerpts. If there is a common chord modulation in which an altered chord is used, indicate its double function.

1. *Sonata for Piano, op. 13* (Beethoven)

2. *String Quartet, op. 18, no. 2* (Beethoven)

3. *Der Doppelganger, from Schwanengesong D. 957* (Schubert)

4. *Sonata for Piano, K. 284* (Mozart)

5. *Waltz for Piano, op. 124, no. 4* (Schumann)

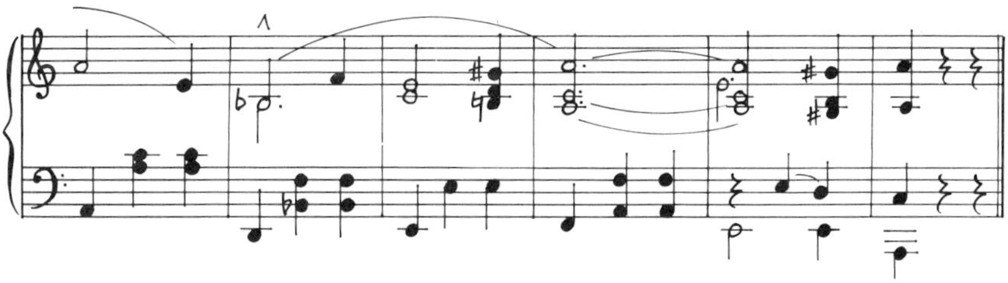

6. *Variations on an Original Theme, op. 36* (Elgar)

7. The German augmented sixth chord in G is ____________
F is ____________
D is ____________
a is ____________
b is ____________
e is ____________

8. The Italian augmented sixth chord in F is ____________
B♭ is ____________
E♭ is ____________
d is ____________
g is ____________
c is ____________

9. The French augmented sixth chord in A is ____________
D is ____________
E is ____________
f♯ is ____________
e is ____________
c♯ is ____________

10. Write all three augmented sixth chords in the following keys. Label each chord and use proper accidentals.

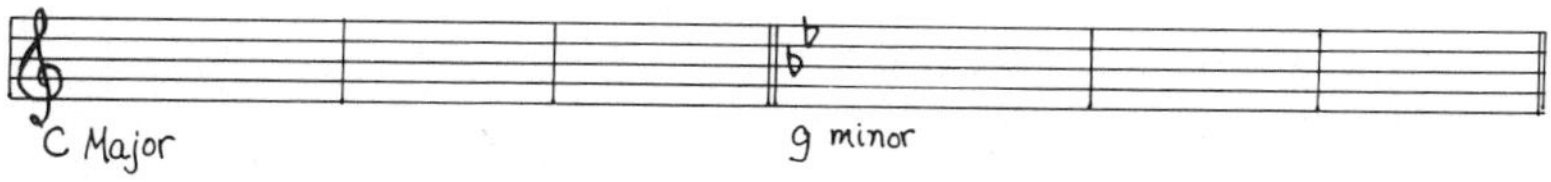

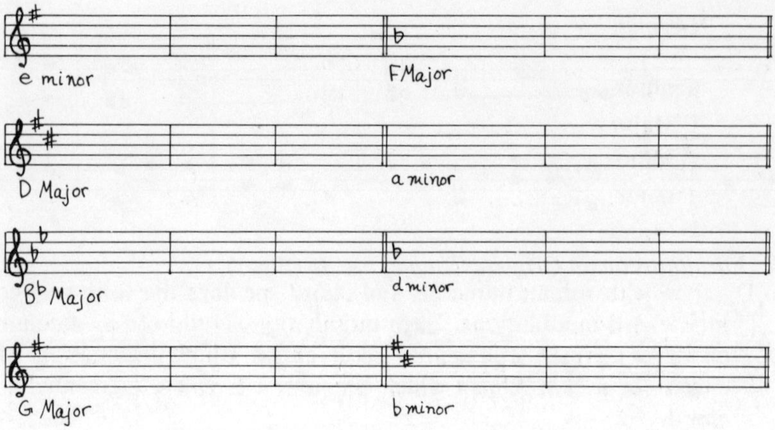

Spell the indicated altered chords in the given key centers:

11. *Secondary Dominants*

V^7/IV in D________	VII^7/IV in b________
V^7/V in G________	VII/II in E♭ ________
V/II in f________	VII^7/III in A________
VII/III in B♭ ________	VII/VI in F________
VII/V in a________	VII^7 in d________

12. *Neapolitan*

D Major________	c minor________
f minor________	G Major________
E♭ Major________	E Major________
a minor________	b minor________
F Major________	d minor________

13. *Augmented Sixth Chords*

Italian	*French*
d minor________	c minor________
A Major________	B♭ Major________
E♭ Major________	g minor________
B♭ Major________	E♭ Major________
g minor________	A Major________

German

a minor_____________
E Major_____________
G Major_____________
e minor_____________
D Major_____________

14. Diagram with roman numerals and chord spellings the following common chord modulations. Each modulation should use as a common chord a German augmented sixth chord which becomes a Mm^7 chord—or a Mm^7 chord which becomes a German augmented sixth chord.

G Major	to	F Major
B♭ Major	to	B Major
d minor	to	A♭ Major

15. Sightsinging practice should include singing all three augmented sixth chords in a given key center: upwards from the root of each chord to the V chord of the key sung upwards from the root; and upwards from the third of each chord to the V chord of the key sung upwards from the root.

Listening Assignment

Beethoven. *String Quartet* in G Major, op. 18, no. 2

Schubert. *An Sylvia*

Wagner. *Tristan und Isolde,* Love-Death

Composition

B♭ Major; $\frac{3}{2}$ time

I | Fr | V^7 | VI | It. | VII^7/V | V^7 III^9 | I ||

c minor; $\frac{4}{8}$ time

I | VII/IV | IV^7 | Gr.
D♭ : V^7 | VI | VII^7/V | V | I ||

Melodies for the above compositions can emphasize the chromaticism made possible by the use of these altered chords. Are your melodies singable?

XV. Impressionism
Aesthetic Principles; Unifying Devices

Although many musicians feel that impressionistic music is in many ways an extension of 19th century romanticism, the impressionists used a mixture of new and old techniques that resulted in special kinds of sounds that are associated with their philosophy of art.

As in other periods of musical development, strong similarities are apparent in the creative efforts of both the visual and musical artists. The paintings of Renoir, Monet and Degas and the music of Debussy and Ravel have been described in the same terms—subjective rather than objective, subtle, vague, hazy, indistinct, suggestive.

Both new and older scale formations were used by the impressionists. The whole tone scales in Example 118 were used in conjunction with pentatonic scales (which were projections of perfect fifths) and certain modal scales.

Example 118

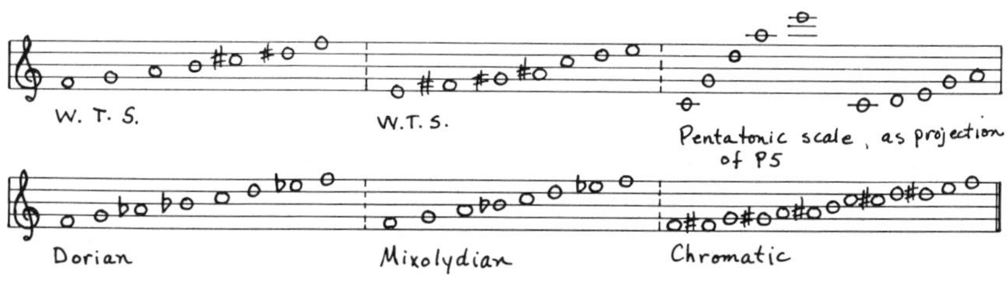

Enharmonically only two whole tone scales are possible since together both six note scales include all the chromatic possibilities. In a real sense these scales are perfect material to create impressionistic music. The direct forceful motion of the normal progression of chords is eliminated because these scales have no perfect fourth, perfect fifth or leading tone. The symmetrical structure of the whole tone scale, the chromatic scale, the augmented triad (a ladder of major thirds) and the diminished seventh chord (a ladder of minor thirds) seem ideally suited for the "nonfunctional" harmony now desired in preference to the usual progression of chords towards a tonal center.

With the "new" whole tone scales are found the older pentatonic and chromatic scales as well as modal scales (see Example 118).

If traditional progressions of functional harmony were to be avoided, what other unifying devices were employed? The feeling for tonal center was enhanced by the use of pedal and the imposition of pentatonic structures. Unifying elements also included modified repetition of short motives, ostinato figures and cadential bass movement at critical points. The very phrase structure itself indicated a tonal nucleus without the structure of classified chord progression.

119. Prelude for Piano, Book I, no. 2 (Debussy)

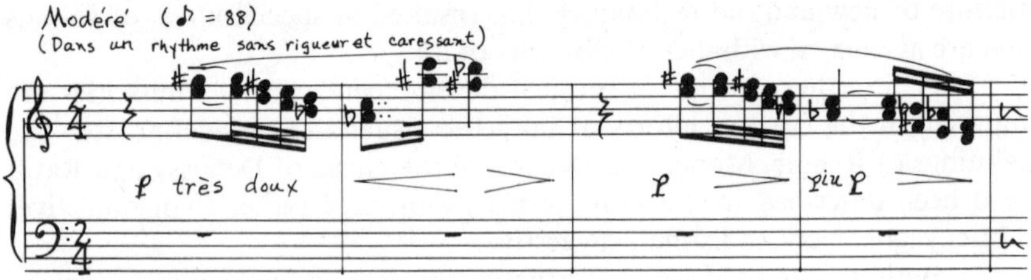

120. Prelude for Piano, Book I, no. 10 (Debussy)

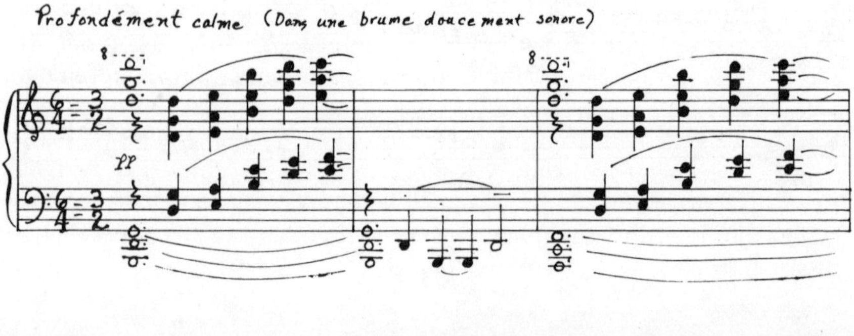

The above examples contain illustrations of the use of the whole tone scale, modified repetitions of short two measure motives and pedal. Example 121 also contains an illustration of another impressionistic technique —planing. Planing is the use of a succession of sonorities usually in parallel motion. Common harmonic structures used in planing are Mm^7, major, minor or augmented triads. Even more complex sonorities such as ninth, eleventh or thirteenth chords are found in the style and serve in their way to make more indistinct the functional harmonies that produce normal chord progressions.

121. Prelude for Piano, Book I, no. 6 (Debussy)

Although Debussy and Ravel are considered in many ways synonymous with impressionism in music there are those differences in style and technique that are always present between individuals. An analysis of Ravel's "Ma Mère l'Oye" clearly shows Ravel's usage of impressionistic techniques.

122. Ma Mère l'Oye: I Pavane de la Belle au bois dormant (Ravel)

Examples 121 and 122:

**These pitches for French Horn in F sound a perfect fifth lower than written (i.e. the first note is concert A).*

123. *Ma Mère l'Oye: II Petit Poucet* (Ravel)

124. *Ma Mère l'Oye: III Laideronnette, Impératrice Jes Pagodes* (Ravel)

125. *Ma Mère l'Oye: V Le Jardin Féerique* (Ravel)

The previous examples illustrate Ravel's usage of the pentatonic scale (Example 122), polymetric signatures with retard to produce an indistinct dimension to meter and parallel planning triads at the cadence (Example 123), long pedals (Example 124) and planning along with pedal (Example 125).

Examples 126 and 127 contain percussive eleventh chords (simply a ladder of thirds above a triad) and an example of the Spanish dance rhythms favored by both Debussy and Ravel.

126. Valses nobles et sentimentales, no. 1 (Ravel)

127. Bolero (Ravel)

The sum total of all of these techniques adds up to a special aurally perceived "color" which is impressionism.

Exercises

1. Write the two whole tone scales along with their enharmonic equivalents.

2. Write five pentatonic scales which do not contain minor seconds.

3. Write mixolydian scales on D, F♯, B and E♭.

4. Sing a sequence of three Mm^7 chords with their roots on B♭, C and D.

5. Sing a sequence of four major triads with their roots on G, A, B and C.

Listening Assignment

Debussy. *Prelude to the Afternoon of a Faun*
Preludes for Piano, Books I and II

Griffes. *The White Peacock*, op. 7, no. 1

Ravel. *Ma Mère l'Oye*
La Valse

Composition

$\frac{4}{4}$ time – 8 measures – Use: Whole tone scale
2 measures modified repetition
pedal

$\frac{9}{8}$ time – 8 measures – Use: Pentatonic scales (projection of perfect fifths)
Planing interludes of Mm^7 chords
2 measures modified repetition
pedal

XVI. 20th Century Meters; Original Scale Formations

It seems that our major efforts in the development of Western music during the 19th century centered around harmonic enrichment. During the same time period metric and melodic aspects were relatively neglected.

Innovative and complex metric emphasis is almost a hallmark of 20th century music. The steady, regular (and sometimes boring) pulse of 18th and 19th century music in $\frac{2}{4}$, $\frac{3}{4}$, $\frac{4}{4}$, $\frac{6}{8}$, or $\frac{9}{8}$ time signatures is replaced in the 20th century by rapidly changing meters in juxtaposition in the same composition—or different meters in different parts at the same time.

Although this new emphasis on meter can be traced into the last quarter of the 19th century, it was 20th century composers such as Igor Stravinsky, Aaron Copland and Béla Bartók who firmly established the new importance to meter.

Here are some of the complex metric structures 20th century composers have been (and are) exploring:

A change in meter than affects only the number of pulses in a measure—and the note-unit that is equal to a pulse is unchanged.

Example 128

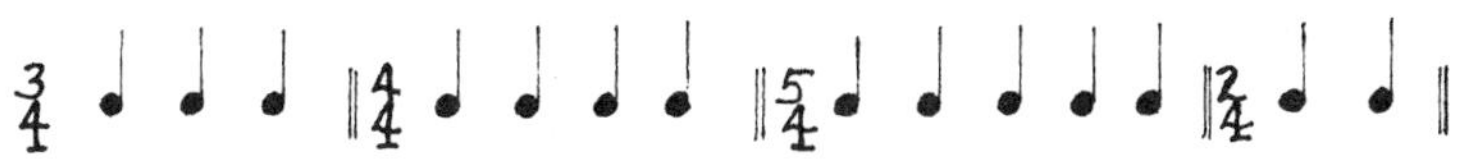

A constant time signature with changing accents.

Example 129

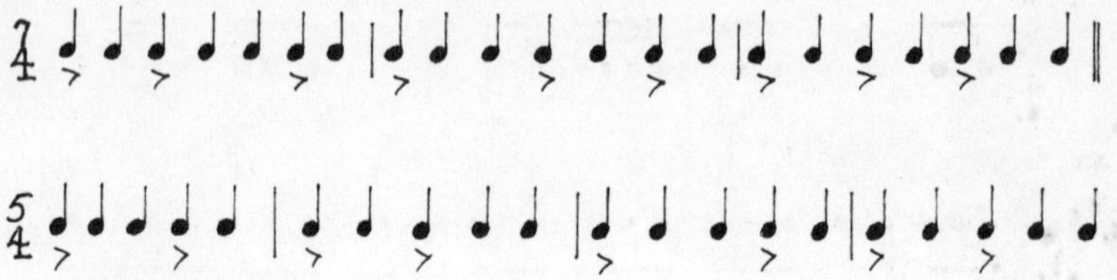

Unusual groupings of pulses within a "usual" time signature.

Example 130

Mixtures of various meters in which the note-units equal to a pulse *are not* the same. Accurate performance depends upon giving the same amount of time to the lowest "common denominator" note value (for example, ♪ in Example 131).

Example 131

Regularly recurring patterns of more than one meter.

Example 132

Different meters in different parts at the same time—polymetric structure.

Example 133

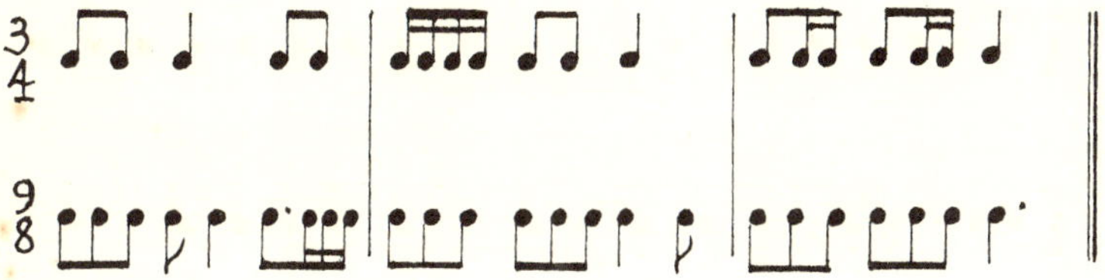

Compositions without time signatures or bar lines with only a general indication of overall tempo and meter.

Example 134

A renewed interest in different melodic material seems to coincide with the emphasis on more complex metric structures. As composers attempted to free themselves of the "tyranny of the bar line" they also developed scale formations other than the traditional major-minor system of the previous centuries.

Besides the whole tone and pentatonic scales used by the impressionists (and others), composers began to investigate folk music sources and to actually develop their own *original* scales to produce intervallic relationships pleasing to them.

Among the new (and sometimes old) scales utilized are those in examples 135 and 136.

135. Hungarian Minor Scale

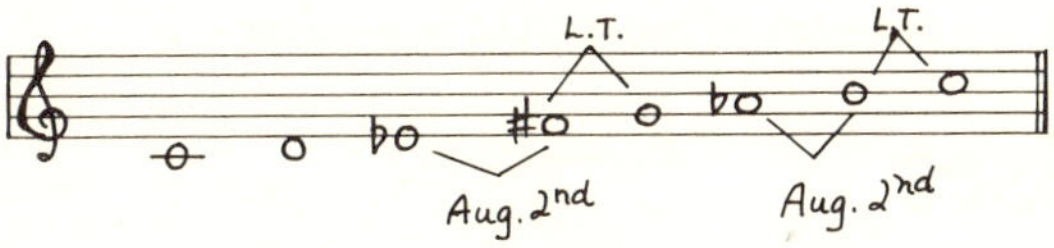

136. Symmetrical Scales

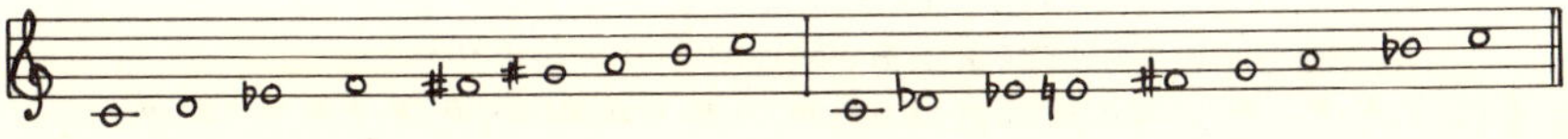

The obvious attraction of the Hungarian minor scale is the "built-in" double leading tones (f♯ to g and b to c) coupled with the two intervals of the augmented second (e♭ to f♯ and a♭ to b). The symmetrical scales alternate whole tone and half tone intervals creating other interesting compositional opportunities.

Example 137

Example 137 illustrates the so-called "mystery chord" of the Russian composer, Alexander Scriabin (1872–1915). The chord, made of various sized fourths, readily adapts itself to scale material.

Example 138

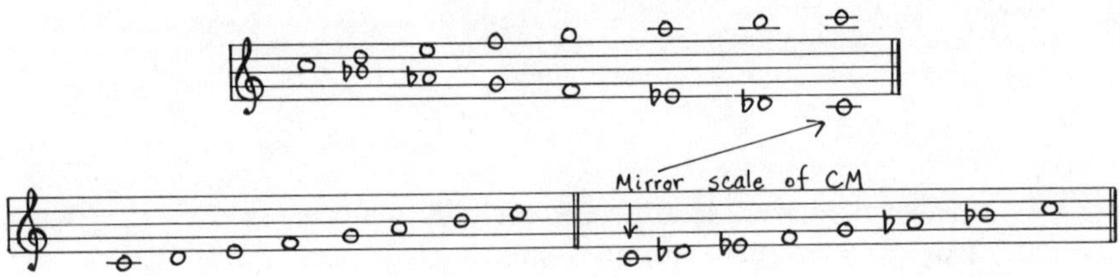

The "mirror scale" produced in Example 138 is derived from the C Major scale by creating the same intervals *downward* from the tonic that produce the familiar major scale pattern *upwards* (i.e. C up to D is a M2; C down to B♭ is a M2; D up to E is a M2; B♭ down to A♭ is a M2, etc.).

A closer look at the mirror scale above reveals its close relationship to the A♭ Major scale—starting and ending on that scale's third step. To utilize this original scale formation in a convincing fashion requires consistent emphasis on the tonic (i.e. C) in terms of repetition and cadence formula. Mirror scales also can be formed from the various types of the minor scale and, of course, from other original scales.

Exercises

1. Write short examples of:
   Unusual groupings of pulses in $\frac{6}{8}$; in $\frac{3}{4}$
   Mixed meter with the ♪ as a common denominator;
   with the 𝅘𝅥𝅯 as a common denominator

2. Write mirror scales based on:

   d harmonic minor
   g melodic minor (ascending)
   e natural minor
   E♭ Major

3. Create an original scale which emphasizes the interval of an A2; contains no P4.

4. Sing the triads produced by the diatonic notes of the mirror scale in Example 138.

5. What is the scale material that forms the melodic basis for this composition? What kind of scale is it?

Prelude for Piano, op. 74, no. 3 (Scriabin)

dim.
cresc.
subito
cresc.
f
f

Listening Assignment

Bartók. *Concerto for Orchestra*
Sonata for 2 Pianos and Percussion

Copland. *Appalachian Spring*

Scriabin. *Preludes for Piano*, op. 74

Stravinsky. *The Rite of Spring*

Composition

1. Use the mirror scale formation in Example 138 and mixed meter similar to Example 131 in a brief song-like passage.

2. Use the Scriabin "mystery chord" scale formation in a short, slow melodious composition (see Example 137).

In order to successfully utilize these original scales, it is important to emphasize the tonic through repetition, durational stress and the "invention" of a cadence formula that "sounds right." In the mirror scale, a V–I cadence produces the traditional interval of a descending fifth between chord roots, but the V is a diminished triad. Obviously, other cadence formulas are possible and practical.

Another distinctive characteristic of this mirror scale is the m2 between tonic and supertonic (i.e., the second step of the scale). If the use of this scale indicates a preference for this intervallic relationship, then the melodic line should emphasize I and II in the scale.

XVII. Quartal Harmony
Three and Four Part Vertical Sonorities

In the search for new ways to tell us their musical message, 20th century composers are exploring nontraditional vertical structures. Instead of the customary triads (three pitches a third apart), vertical sonorities can be built by superimposed fourths.

Example 139

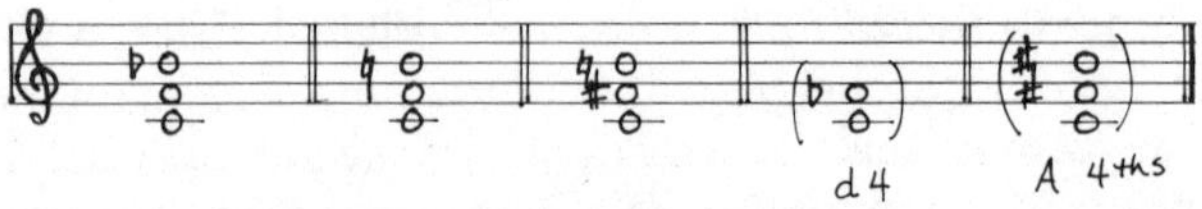

The quartal structures in Example 139 are formed by combining various kinds of fourths. The first chord contains two P4; the second chord a P4 and an A4; the third chord an A4 and a P4. The diminished fourth (d4) is not generally used in this context because it sounds like a M3 and, of course, that is the "old" interval to be replaced. A combination of two A4's is usually avoided since B♯ and C sound like the octave.

Other interesting sounds are derived when we take these same structures and invert them.

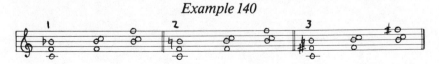

Example 140

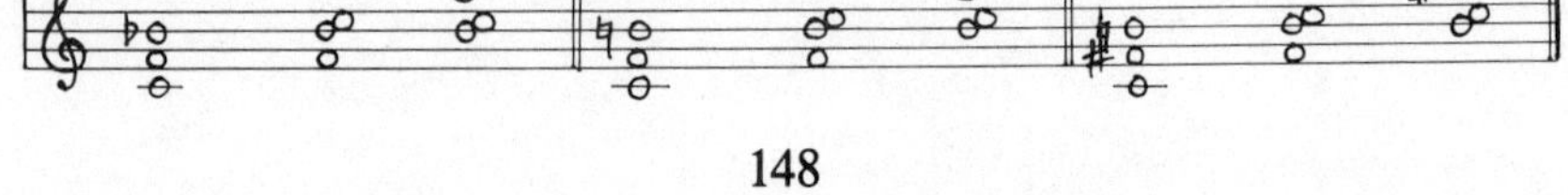

The first quartal structure in Example 140 (a projection of two P4) gives us the M2 and P5 when inverted as well as the P4 and m7 of the original chord. The second quartal structure (a projection of a P4 and an A4) gives us a m2 and P5 when inverted as well as the P4, A4 and M7 of the original chord. The third quartal structure (a projection of an A4 and a P4) gives us m2, d5, and P5 when inverted as well as the A4, P4 and M7 of the original chord.

Example 141

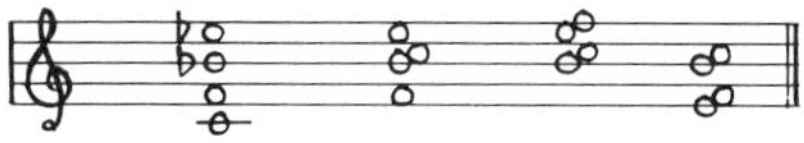

Example 141 illustrates four note projections of the P4 with inversions. Besides the P4s, the m7, and m3 (c–e♭) are present in the original chord. The inversions of the chord add the M2, P5 and M6 to the inventory of possible intervallic relationships.

Because quartal chords can sound like incomplete ninth or thirteenth chords, it is important to use them so that the fourths are prominently heard. After all, 20th century composers are attracted to these sonorities precisely because a contrast to triadic harmonies is desired.

142. Bagatelle, op. 6, no. 11 (Bartók)

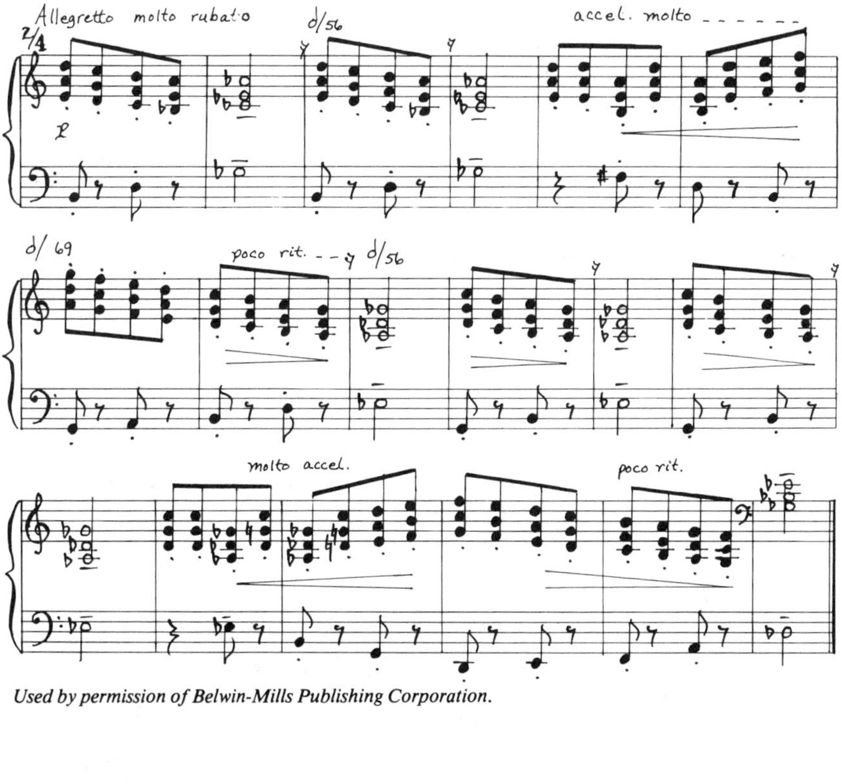

143. *Nocturne (1950)* (Joseph Bein)

Used by permission of the composer.

144. *King David: Introduction* (Honegger)

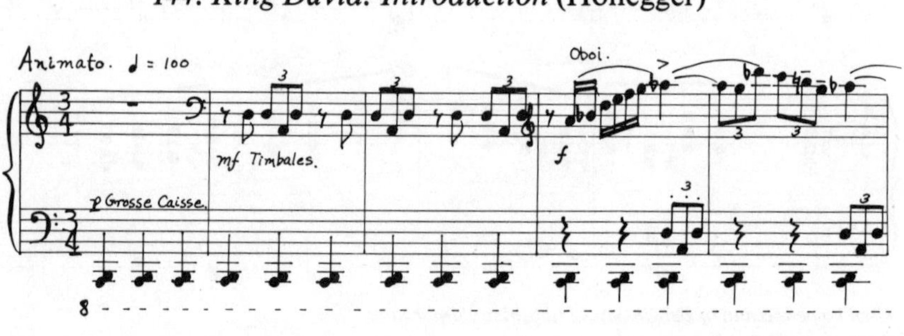

8
tr
8
f
f
Più lento. ♩ = 56.
Oboi
dimin.

The three preceding examples contain compositions in which quartal sonorities are made obvious. Note that melodic material can *also* emphasize fourths (Example 143) or use entirely different material (Example 144) based either on traditional or nontraditional scales.

It is rare to find a complete composition exclusively devoted to quartal sonorities. Composers tend to write sections of longer compositions using these sounds or intersperse quartal sonorities with traditional triadic structures.

Because three and four note quartal chords can have ambiguous roots (such as equidistant sonorities like the augmented triad or the d^7) the emphasis on a pitch center at cadences can be developed for the listener by some simple, obvious techniques.

The pitch center—whether it be a single pitch or a vertical sonority of some complexity—can be established as a center or point of repose by repetition, duration, use of the pedal, volume, or a "cadence formula" (any two- or three-chord progression favored by the composer) repeatedly used. Of course, these techniques are available in addition to the usual progression of chords that traditionally form the cadence.

Exercises

1. Give three kinds of intervallic arrangements of three-note chords by fourths.

2. Using P4, give fundamental, first and second inversions (within the octave) of the following chords built on:

3. Sing the completed exercises above. Choose pitches at random and sing three note chords above them made from various kinds of fourths.

4. Analyze the following musical excerpt. What scale forms the melody? What is the basis of the harmonic structure? How is the cadence formed?

Ma Mère l'Oye: III Laideronnette (Ravel)

Listening Assignment

Honegger. *King David*

Ravel. *Sheherazade*

Walton. *Belshazzar's Feast*

Composition

1. Using the following metric design, compose a singable melody which emphasizes fourths and is supported by quartal sonorities.

♩ = 126

$$\begin{matrix}6\\8\end{matrix}\;\Big\|\;\begin{matrix}3\\4\end{matrix}\;\Big\|\;\begin{matrix}5\\8\end{matrix}\;\Big\|\;\begin{matrix}3\\8\end{matrix}\;\Big\|\;\begin{matrix}3\\4\end{matrix}\;\Big\|\;\begin{matrix}4\\8\end{matrix}\;\Big\|\;\begin{matrix}1\\8\end{matrix}\;\Big\|\;\begin{matrix}6\\8\end{matrix}\;\Big\|$$

2. Using quartal structures interspersed with triadic material, compose approximately eight measures in traditional metric design with an original scale as the basis for the melody.

XVIII. Polytonality
Structure and Function

A long view of the evolution of Western music since the last quarter of the 19th century indicates that composers have been (and are) developing new concepts of tonality.

On the one hand we hear the gradual expansion of the seven note scale to complete chromaticism—a tonal center that encompasses all twelve divisions of the octave. Previous chapters have dealt with these techniques (for instance, altered chords, modulation, etc.).

Another concept seems to be the conscious rejection of a tonal center—an idea to be explored in Chapter XIX.

A third direction entails the use of more than one tonal center at the same time—*polytonality*. The idea of more than one tonal center may or may not be implied by the use of *polychords* (that is, the combination of two or more different sonorities—CM and E♭M triads)—even for an extended time span.

One of the better known examples of a polychord is the famous "Petrouchka" chord which utilizes both the CM and F♯M triads. Example 145 clearly illustrates Stravinsky's simultaneous use of the CM and F♯M triads. Because the timbre, pitch range and metric figures are the same in both voices (Stravinsky uses two clarinets in the orchestration), the impression of two tonal centers is probably not intended.

The excerpts from compositions by Charles Ives and Arthur Honegger in examples 146 and 147 seem to indicate that the composers intend that the listener be aware of more than one tonal center. Both excerpts introduce different tonal centers at different times with different timbres (or dynamic

145. *Petrouchka, Scene 2* (Stravinsky)

levels) with different pitch ranges and with different metric structures. Both composers use widely separated key centers. Ives uses D♭M and FM and Honegger uses A, B♭M, and G♭M.

146. *Variations on "America," first interlude* (Ives)

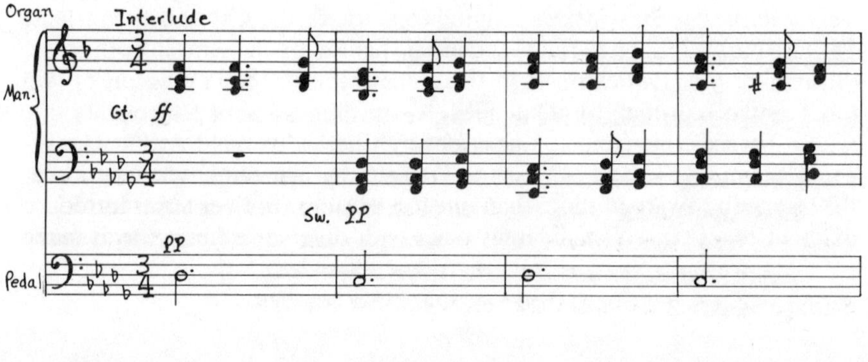

147. King David, third fanfare (Honegger)

Certain techniques are used to give the impression of polytonality:

The use of tonal centers with widely different key signatures, affording a minimal opportunity to use the same pitch in more than one tonal center.

Once the tonal centers have been selected, a clear scale formation is maintained (that is, the use of "extra" notes is avoided).

Each tonal center is established before another is added.

Tonal centers are well separated in "pitch space." For example, one center might be high in the treble staff and another might be mid-range in the bass staff.

Tonal centers use different meters, rhythmic figures, dynamic levels and timbre. For example, a lively melodic line at the *f* level for an orchestral instrument might be used with a second center containing chords for piano at the *p* level in a different meter, with still another center using a pedal or repeated bass line figure in longer note values for bass guitar played *ff*.

Various kinds of tonal centers can be combined. Using major, minor and pentatonic centers with symmetrical, mirror and other original scales is practical and desirable. Example 148 illustrates some possibilities.

Example 148

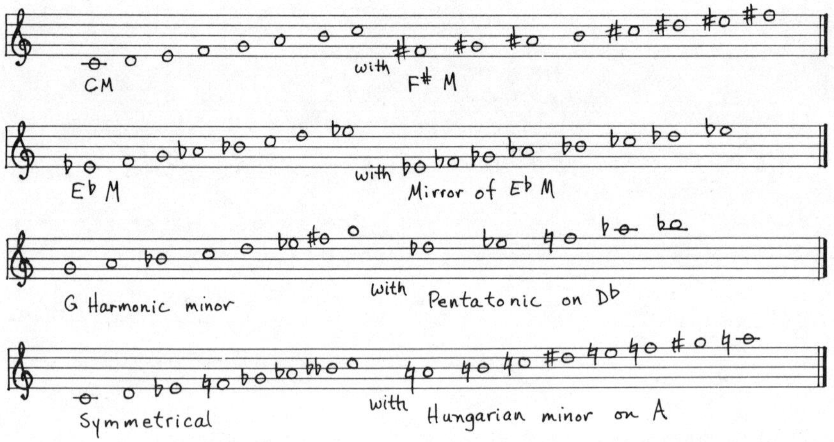

Exercises

1. Write three combinations of at least two different scale formations that will "work" to produce polytonal effects.

2. Write three combinations of at least two different metric formations that will "work" to produce polytonal effects.

3. Write a series of polychords that (a) use similar metric figures; (b) use different metric figures but do not promote polytonality.

4. Sing the melodic lines in Examples 145 and 147 and the Bartók *Bagatelle* that follows.

5. Sing the following scales beginning on C

   Major
   harmonic minor
   melodic minor
   Hungarian minor
   pentatonic (P5 projection)

6. Sing the scales as above on E, on B♭.

7. In the following example by Milhaud: What are the tonal centers? How are the centers different in musical content? What is the musical "sense" to the halfnotes in the bass?

Saudades do Brazil: no. 7, Corcovado (Milhaud)

Reprinted with the permission of Editions Max Eschig, Paris.

8. Play or listen to a recording of the *Bagatelle*, op. 6, no. 1 by Bartók. Are you aware of two tonal centers? Why? Why not? Does the composition close with a single center or more than one center? What scale formations are employed?

Bagatelle, op. 6, no. 1 (Bartók)

Used by permission of Belwin-Mills Publishing Corporation.

Listening Assignment

Stravinsky. *Petrouchka*

Bartók. *Bagatelle,* op. 6, no. 1

Milhaud. *Saudades do Brazil*

Ives. *Variations on America*

Composition

Write approximately eight measures of a polytonal setting in mixed meter at a slow tempo. Use as many techniques as seem practical from the listing in this chapter after Example 147.

XIX. 12-Tone and Serial Composition

Tone Rows; Derivatives and Serial Expansion

Atonality—the conscious rejection of a tonal center—can be achieved whether or not a 12-tone technique is utilized. And, as we shall hear, tonal centers can be emphasized even with the use of a 12-tone technique.

First, then, what is atonal music? Generally speaking it has abandoned the traditional functionalism (i.e., second class to first class to tonic) of individual pitches and chords within a tonal center to the point where a feeling for "home-base" is lost. There is no psychological gravitation to any particular sound or sounds.

The 12-tone composition is a systematic procedure by which all the pitch material (melodic and harmonic) for a composition can be derived from a single arrangement of the 12 tones within the octave.

To many musicians this "method of composing with 12 tones" developed by Arnold Schoenberg in the 1920's was the logical evolution of the expansion of chromaticism in the late 19th century. The major and minor scales seemed to be replaced with just one—the chromatic scale. Furthermore, Schoenberg considered all 12 pitches of the chromatic scale of equal importance with no emphasis on the tonic, dominant or other pitches in the major–minor system.

To compose in the 12-tone technique, the 12 tones of the chromatic scale are arranged in a *tone row* or sequence so that those intervals important to the composer are utilized. Since this system was intended to avoid tonality, the tone row is usually constructed without suggestions of triads or other reminders of "the old system."

Once the original tone row (O) has been developed, three other forms

Once the original tone row (O) has been developed, three other forms of the row are immediately available: I (inversion)—the O (original) upside down; R (retrograde)—the O backwards; and RI (the retrograde of the inversion)—the inversion backwards. If we were developing a row of numbers, the four forms of the row would look like:

O–1	2	3	4	5	6	7	8	9	10	11	12
I– Ɩ	ᄅ	Ɛ	ㄣ	ϛ	9	ㄥ	8	6	0Ɩ	ƖƖ	ᄅƖ
R–12	11	10	9	8	7	6	5	4	3	2	1
RI–ᄅƖ	ƖƖ	0Ɩ	6	8	ㄥ	9	ϛ	ㄣ	Ɛ	ᄅ	Ɩ

149. Three Songs, op. 23 (Webern)

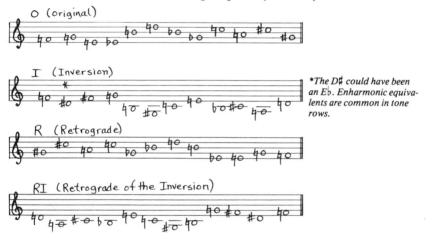

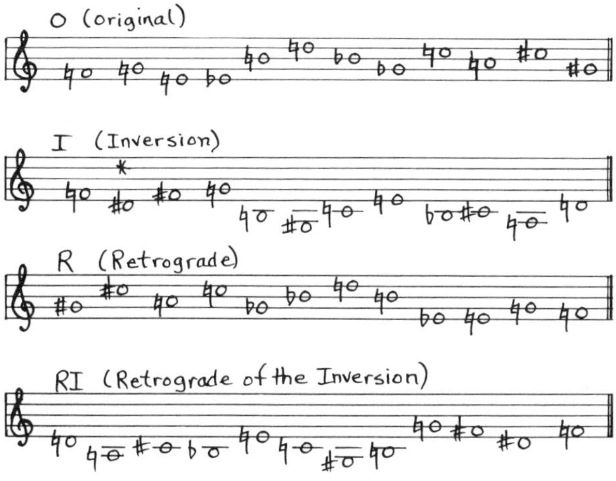

**The D♯ could have been an E♭. Enharmonic equivalents are common in tone rows.*

Example 149 illustrates the four basic forms of the tone row Anton Webern (a student of Arnold Schoenberg) used in his *Three Songs*, opus 23. Notice that I begins on the same pitch as O and duplicates each interval of O in the opposite direction. The R is O from last pitch to first pitch in order. the RI is I from last pitch to first pitch in order.

Each pitch is identified by an accidental merely as a practical aid in performance. Although this practice adds to the tasks of the composer, it seems to be time and effort well spent in terms of good performance.

The four tone rows can be transposed to any other pitch in the chromatic scale. For example, O could begin F♯, G♯, E♯, E♮ etc.—one semitone higher. The transposed row would be named O:1, indicating its position of one semitone above the "O:0." Similarly, O:4 would read A♮, B♮, G♯, G♮ etc.—indicating a reproduction of O four semitones higher; R:3 would begin on B♮—three semitones higher; RI:2 would begin on E♮—two semitones higher, etc.

In other words, all four forms of the tone row can begin on any of the 12 pitches of the chromatic scale—a total of 48 possible forms of one row. This considerable amount of compositional material is often difficult to remember. As a memory aid (and working tool) many composers develop a tone row matrix for easier accessibility.

One form of a tone row matrix is shown in Example 150. It is based upon the tone rows in Example 149. The pitches that form O:0 are written across the top; the pitches of I:0 are written down the left side. The matrix is completed with the transpositions of O. The matrix is used by reading from left to right for the 12 forms of O; reading from right to left for the 12 forms of R; reading from top to bottom for the 12 forms of I; reading from bottom to top for the 12 forms of RI.

150. Tone Row Matrix

	I:0 ↓												
O:0 →	F♮	G♮	E♮	E♭	B♮	D♮	B♭	G♭	C♮	A♭	C♯	G♯	← R:0
	D♯	F♮	D♮	D♭	A♮	C♮	A♭	E♮	B♭	G♮	B♮	F♯	
	F♯	G♯	F♮	E♮	C♮	D♯	B♮	G♮	C♯	A♯	D♮	A♮	
	G♮	A♮	F♯	F♮	C♯	E♮	C♮	A♭	D♮	B♮	D♯	A♯	
	B♮	C♯	B♭	A♮	F♮	A♭	E♮	C♮	G♭	E♭	G♮	D♮	
	G♯	A♯	G♮	G♭	D♮	F♮	C♯	A♮	D♯	C♮	E♮	B♮	
	C♮	D♮	B♮	B♭	F♯	A♮	F♮	D♭	G♮	E♮	G♯	D♯	
	E♮	F♯	E♭	D♮	B♭	D♭	A♮	F♮	B♮	A♭	C♮	G♮	
	B♭	C♮	A♮	A♭	E♮	G♮	E♭	C♭	F♮	D♮	F♯	C♯	
	C♯	D♯	B♯	B♮	G♮	A♯	F♯	D♮	G♯	E♯	A♮	E♮	
	A♮	B♮	G♯	G♮	D♯	F♯	D♮	B♭	E♮	C♯	E♯	C♮	
	D♮	E♮	C♯	C♮	G♯	B♮	G♮	E♭	A♮	F♯	A♯	E♯	
	↑ RI:0												

When tonality was the only composition structure in use, there were certain basic procedures followed by composers to make it operate successfully. Now that the new 12-tone technique is also available, certain other basic procedures are generally adhered to:

The tone row (in any form) must be used completely in sequence (melodically) or vertically (harmonically) and any pitch can be used in any octave. At times, a segment or segments of the row may be used successively. Exceptions: trills, tremolos and repetitions (of single notes) are generally allowed.

Metric, melodic (use of pitches in any octave) and dynamic innovation is highly prized.

Two or more forms of the tone row may be used together.

Examples 151 and 152 illustrate the musical use of tone rows by two different composers. The original tone row for *Descant* (for unaccompanied clarinet) by Cheslock is reproduced immediately above the music. The composition begins with three statements of O as indicated. The 16th note passage in measure 10 (which is circled) interrupts O with a 12-tone row of different origin. Measure 11, however, continues with two more statements of O. A retrograde (R) begins in measure 17 to be interrupted again (in measure 20) by the same row used in measure 10 but, transposed down a semitone. Measure 21 continues with two more statements of R. The rows in this com-

151. Descant (Cheslock)

From Descant for Unaccompanied Clarinet *by Louis Cheslock.*

position are relatively easy to analyze although each statement of the row is different melodically (because of the use of different octaves) and metrically. Notice that the row does not necessarily correspond to the musical phrases.

Schoenberg's use of the row shown in Example 152 is a bit more complicated. The use of the tone row is illustrated in the beginnings of three of the movements of the *Suite* both melodically and harmonically. For ease in analysis, the pitches of the row are numbered. The bass line of the *Praeludium* is a d5 from O (i.e. six semitones from O)—it would be labeled O:6. Notice the three groups of four notes that make up this row. The row in the *Gavotte* is not in sequence so we can assume the composer preferred to use segments of the row as entities. The first measure of the *Gigue* is a "textbook" example of the use of the row vertically and horizontally.

152. *Suite for Piano, op. 25* (Schoenberg)

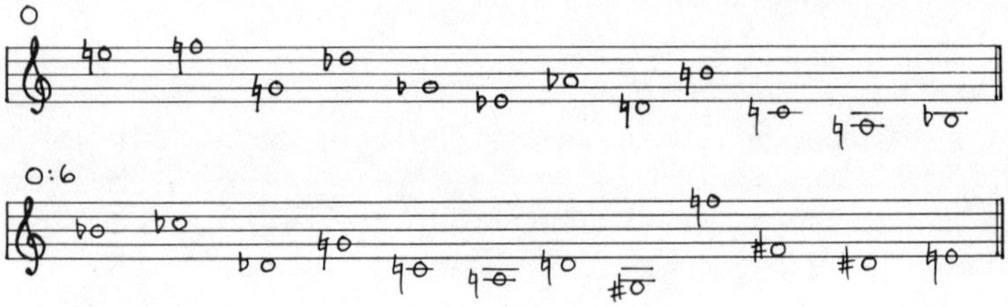

Praeludium

Gavotte

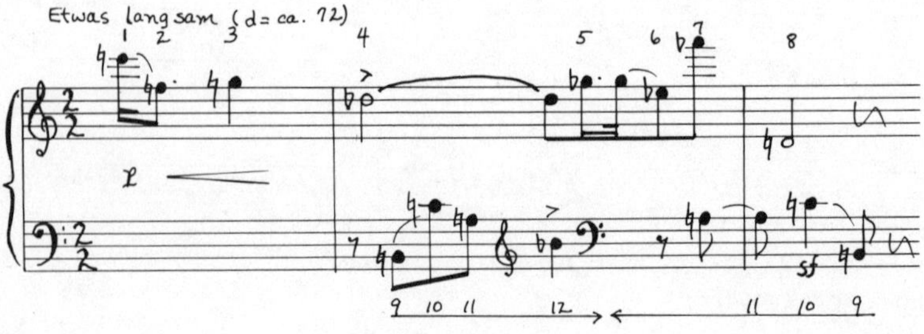

Gigue

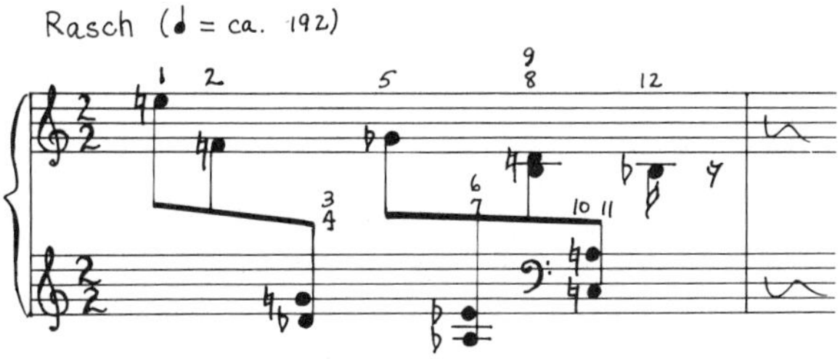

Used by permission of Belmont Music Publishers, Los Angeles, California 90049.

The vertical (i.e. harmonic) use of the row in segments presents the pitches in the original sequence but simultaneously. The segments are considered as chords in this style.

Another illustration of the melodic and harmonic use of the row is contained in the first four measures of another Schoenberg composition shown in Example 153. The sequence of the row in the bass clef seems to indicate again the composer's use of the row in segments. In this case, the second half of the row is used (a hexachord—six pitches). Other divisions of the row into groups of three or four pitches are common.

153. Pieces for Piano, op. 23, no. 5 (Schoenberg)

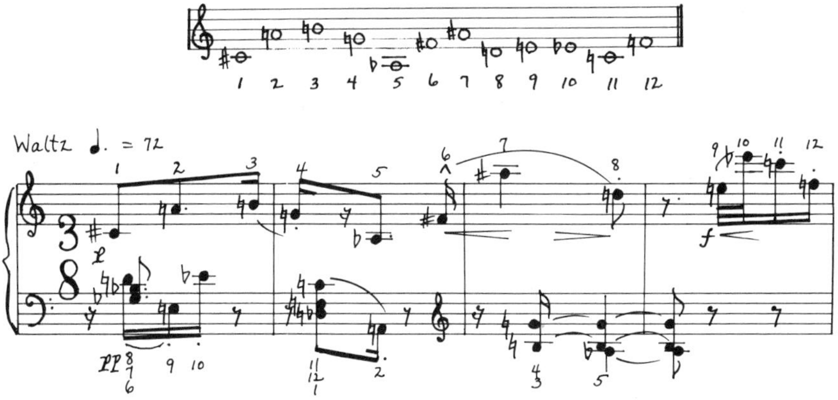

Used by permission of Belmont Music Publishers, Los Angeles, California 90049.

The construction of a tone row can—if the composer chooses—indicate strong tonal tendencies. The tone row Alban Berg (another student of Schoenberg) designed for his *Violin Concerto* is reproduced in Example 154, on the next page.

154. Violin Concerto tone row (Berg)

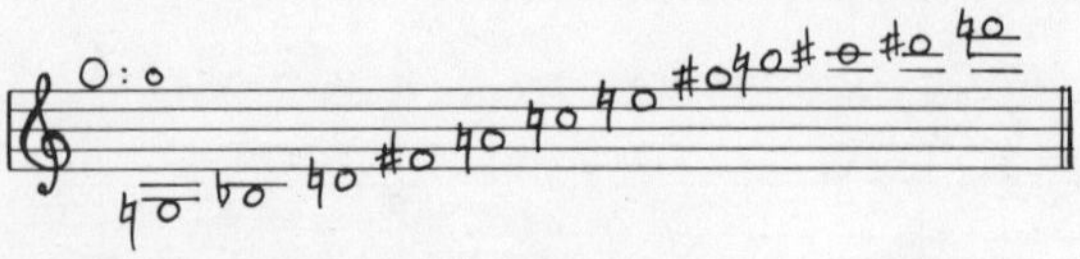

The series of triads and four pitches an M2 apart (at the end of the row) are used with strong tonal suggestions.

In fact, composers can (and do) create a feeling for "center" within the context of 12-tone technique rather readily. The simple musical tasks of using additional duration, repetition, dynamic stress and any original "cadence formula" effectively creates a feeling for "center" for any single pitch or sonority.

Although this discussion of tone rows has been exclusively about *12*-tone technique, 20th century composers use tone rows of varying lengths—rows of five, six or eight tones are not uncommon. In all tone row composition, however, as in all other styles of composition, the technique is a means to a musical end. And in many compositions that end is best served by "breaking the rules." The row and its derivatives are not "sacred."

Serialism or serial composition refers to the adaptation of 12-tone technique to all other aspects of musical composition. Dynamics, timbre, tempo, meter or any other factor in making music can be ordered in much the same way as pitch. All that is necessary is the construction of a series of 12 dynamic levels, or 12 articulations or 12 tempos and the "row" can be placed in a matrix (see Example 150). In other words, it is possible to predetermine all aspects of the composition—before the first measure is written. The development of serialism is one of the important factors that led to electronic music—the topic of the next chapter.

Exercises

1. Develop a tone row that emphasizes a particular interval. Write the I, R and RI forms of this row. Construct a pitch matrix.

2. Develop a tone row that emphasizes as many different intervals as possible. Write the O:4 and O:6 forms of this row.

3. Sing the O forms of the two rows you have just created. Sing the Křenek composition that follows.

4. Write the O form of the row used in the following composition (it is the

first 12 pitches in the "right hand"). Analyze the construction of both "lines" of the composition in terms of this original form of the row.

Eight Piano Pieces, no. 1, Etude (Křenek)

5. The row for the following composition is in the first violin part. How are the vertical sonorities ("sets of three") related to this row?

Fourth String Quartet, op. 37 (Schoenberg)

Used by permission of Belmont Music Publishers, Los Angeles, California 90049.

Listening Assignment

Berg. *Concerto for Violin and Orchestra*

Schoenberg. *Five Pieces for Piano,* op. 23
Suite for Piano, op. 25
Fourth String Quartet, op. 37

Webern. *Passacaglia for Orchestra,* op. 1

Composition

1. Write a single line 12-tone composition using as much melodic, dynamic and metric innovation as seems reasonable. Construct O, I, R and RI of the row before you begin the composition. Attempt to build your row with few (or no) "reminders" of tonality.

2. Create a short piece which uses a tone row slightly suggestive of some aspects of tonality. The row (and its derivatives) should be used both melodically and harmonically. Consider using segments of the row (i.e., groups of three, four or six consecutive pitches) in a systematic way. Construct O, I, R and RI of the row before you begin the composition.

XX. Electronic Music
Musique Concrete; The Uses of Tape Recorders and Synthesizers

Given the propensity of 20th century composers to search for new and different ways to express themselves, the advent of electronic music was almost inevitable. As soon as the equipment was available, new techniques for making music were developed.

Perhaps one had better first define "electronic music": it does not mean mechanically amplified sound such as an amplified guitar in a rock group. It does not mean a modified traditional musical instrument such as an electric organ or electronic church bells. These developments arose to provide substitute instruments when financial and/or spatial considerations were primary. Nor of course does "electronic music" refer to an electromechanical recording of a piece of music.

Electronic music *is* music that is made with the aid of tape recorders, tape splicing equipment, amplifiers, loudspeakers, synthesizers and computers along with the ingenuity and talent of live composers.

Although composers have used and/or imitated natural sounds in their music for a long time, the idea of recording natural sounds (or those produced by ordinary musical instruments) and then *altering* these sounds is a technique belonging exclusively to the 20th century.

The manipulation of taped natural sounds is *musique concrète*. That is, the source of the sounds occur in nature (car horns, the sounds of animals, the closing of a door, etc.) and in the sounds produced by musical instruments (a single note played by a piano, gong, trumpet, etc.).

What can be done to change these sounds so that they become "new" material for musical composition? The inventory of "altering techniques" is extensive. For example, the taped sound of a single piano note can be played backwards. The result is much different than the sound we usually associate with the piano. Instead of a strong beginning and a gradually diminuendo, we hear the reverse accompanied by a beginning attack in reverse!

Once sounds have been recorded, the tape can be run through the machine at half speed or double speed or even at variable speeds. The "new" sounds will be altered in pitch, timbre and duration. Altered so extensively, in fact, that the original source may be unrecognizable.

The tape of original natural sounds can be formed into a loop and run through the machine to produce an endless "round" of compositional material. And this loop can be used backwards and at different speeds.

The use of tape recorders also gives us a new dimension in musical time. Instead of relying upon *relative* time values (e.g., 𝅗𝅥 = ♩♩ = ♫♫ etc.) it is possible to measure *absolute* time (the playback speed of the tape can be 7½ inches per second or 15 inches per second, etc.). This new concept enables composers to deal with duration of sound in a very precise way. In other words, length of tape equals duration.

Now that the composer has created new sound sources, the next task in the creative process is to arrange these sounds into a musical shape. Usually this involves the use of a tape splicing mechanism. Since the tapes of these various sounds can be cut, rearranged and spliced together in an enless variety of combinations, the composer is free to develop innovative sequences. Furthermore, he can produce intricate and involved metric patterns thanks to the exactness made possible with tape splicing techniques. And tapes can be rerecorded on top of each other. This multi-layer of sounds can be a sound source in itself.

The taped composition can be further modified by regulating volume patterns and stereophonic effects. When completed, the tape composition is ready for performance. It can either be transferred to a commercial record or "performed" directly through an amplifier and loudspeakers—in either case without the musical functions usually supplied by a performer. The traditional triumvirate of composer–performer–listener has become simply composer–listener.

The *synthesizer* can further aid the composer when used with the tape recorder and tape splicing mechanism. The synthesizer is an electronic machine that can produce sounds of any pitch, volume, timbre and duration desired. If the composer wishes a sound with 441 vibrations per second instead of one with 440 vibrations per second, the synthesizer will oblige. If a sound is desired whose timbre is controlled by strong sixth, seventh and eighth partials—or weaker third, fifth and seventh partials—or no upper partials at all—the synthesizer will respond with the twist of a dial.* The synthesizer can also produce complicated series of varying pitches, timbres, dynamics and metric combinations. All in all, the synthesizer replaces

**See Chapter II for a review of the overtone series which controls the timbre of any sound.*

musique concrète with electronically produced sounds which can be controlled with remarkable precision by the composer.

The new sounds produced by the synthesizer must now be recorded on tape and the complex tasks of splicing commenced to produce a musical result.

The use of the computer is the next logical step in the escalation of electronic music machines. Since any sound—no matter how complex—can be "described" to a computer, a computerized musical vocabulary can be developed. Eventually, the computer can—upon request—produce any desired sound, sequence of pitches or metric patterns, or can develop musical options or even make choices for the composer.

The present state of the art is such that a composer can enter a computer center with a notebook in hand and leave the computer center with a tape recording of a completed composition forever ready for the listener (without reference to the musical skills of the performer).

A modification of pure electronic music is the combination of a tape and a live performer (or performers). The tape can be prepared from either musique concrète or electronic sources (or a combination of both). The demands upon the live performer, however, are quite different from the musical situation that does not use tape. Instead of the typical give-and-take among live performers in playing a traditional composition, the performers now must make all the adjustments to the tape in meter, dynamics, intonation, etc.

What sort of music is electronic music? Just as "piano music" can mean the classicism of Mozart or the romanticism of Chopin or the serialism of Webern, electronic music can mean many different kinds of music.

The electronic music composer can develop a collage of various types and layers of sound sources. Or the composition may be made of many different sources placed in juxtaposition purely by chance (this is known as "aleatory" music). Or the composition can be based upon electronic sources assembled into traditional musical forms. Or the construction of the composition can be influenced by the physical space in which it is intended to be performed or the number of minutes available on each side of an LP record. Or the composition can be based upon the serialization of the parameters of sound.

The extension of serialism from human performers to electronic sound sources is a musical phenomenon which, in retrospect, was inevitable. In the realization of musical thoughts through the serializations of various components of sound (pitch, volume, timbre, duration), some composers found themselves narrowed by the frailities of the performers and the limitations of musical instruments. A given instrument can only be played in a certain pitch range. If the composer wishes that instrument's timbre to sound either above or below the instrument's pitch range—he is musically limited. Not all musical instruments are "created equal"—some have greater dynamic ranges than others, some are capable of greater technical facility than others, etc. Human performers also are limited in terms of what is technically possible in the areas of dynamic range, physical facility, etc.

The accessibility of electronic sound sources solved the problem of external musical limitations upon the composer. Now the only limitation the composer had to deal with was his own imagination. Literally, any sound—of any pitch; of any timbre; of any dynamic level—imagined by the composer can be produced by electronic sound sources. Any series of sounds—of any speed; of any degree of separation; of any metric complexity—imagined by the composer can be electronically produced. Serialism can reign unfettered.

What do these various kinds of electronic music sound like? The following recordings illustrate one or more of the various techniques (or styles) discussed here. They are all "recommended listening."

Edgard Varèse. *Poèm Electronique*. A composition specifically for performance in a building in the Brussels World Fair (1958). It was intended to be heard through 400 loudspeakers placed within the hall and uses both musique concrète and electronic sound sources.

John Cage. *Aria with Fontana Mix*. This is a contradiction in terms. *Fontana Mix* is intended to be chance (aleatory) music—that is, a collection of various bits and pieces of electronic music to be performed in random sequence. Obviously, once the composition was recorded, the aleatory dimension disappears and it becomes a collage of electronic music. The *Aria* is an improvised vocal composition in many styles. Again the "improvisation" is no more once the composition is recorded.

Mario Davidovsky. *Synchronisms No. 1 for Flute and Tape*. A composition for tape and a live flutist.

Milton Babbitt. *Composition for Synthesizer*. An electronic serialized composition.

Morton Subotnick. *Silver Apples of the Moon*. A composition intended for distribution and performance on an LP record. The sound source is a synthesizer.

Charles Wuorinen. *Time's Encomium*. Both synthesizer and computer generated sound is used in a composition intended for two sides of an LP record.

Exercises

If a tape recorder is available:

1. Record a single note struck on the piano. Play it back at a different speed than that used for the recording. Play it back "backwards" and at different speeds. Notice the difference between playbacks and the original sound.

2. Record random sounds in class—voices, hand claps, coughs, a book dropped on a desk, etc. Play these sounds back at different speeds and backwards.

If a tape recorder and a tape splicer are available:

3. Make choices and develop sounds acceptable as compositional material. By cutting and splicing tape: (A) compose these sounds in a collage lasting 60 seconds; (B) compose these sounds into an A–B–A form lasting 60 seconds.

If a synthesizer is available:

4. Develop an inventory of sounds as varied as your technique will allow.

If a synthesizer, a tape recorder and a tape splicer are available:

5. Record your chosen sounds. By cutting and splicing tape, compose a short composition which includes both musique concrète and synthesizer produced sounds.

Index